W9-BKB-689

Norman Rockwell's PORTRAIT OF AMERICA

Written by Victoria Crenson
Designed by Steve Barber

CRESCENT BOOKS
New York

Illustrations reprinted under license from
the Estate of Norman Rockwell.

Copyright © 1989 Estate of Norman Rockwell

Photographic material courtesy of
The Norman Rockwell Museum at
Stockbridge, Stockbridge, MA

Created and manufactured by arrangement with
Ottenheimer Publishers, Inc.

Copyright © 1989 Ottenheimer Publishers, Inc.
This 1989 edition is published by Ottenheimer
Publishers, Inc. for Crescent Books,
distributed by Crown Publishers, Inc.,
225 Park Avenue South, New York, New York 10003

All rights reserved.

Printed and bound in Hong Kong.

ISBN 0-517-67897-7
h g f e d c b a

Library of Congress Cataloging-in-Publication Data

Rockwell, Norman, 1894–1978.
    Norman Rockwell's America : portrait of America.
    p.   cm.
    Includes index.
    ISBN 0-517-67897-7
    1. Rockwell, Norman, 1894–1978 — Themes, motives.   2. United States
in art.   I. Title.   II. Title: Portrait of America.
ND237.R68A4   1989a
759.13—dc20

CONTENTS

Breaking Home Ties (1954)

INTRODUCTION

For six decades, through two World Wars, the Great Depression, unprecedented national prosperity and radical social change, Norman Rockwell held a mirror up to America and reflected its identity through the portraits he painted of its people. Rockwell painted real people—freckles, wrinkles, big ears and all—and, like an art director, he staged entire scenes, creating settings and suggesting situations for them. His work, as reproduced on millions of magazine covers, proved to be arresting on the newsstands, and established a distinctive look for **The Saturday Evening Post** that was a major factor in its popularity. But Rockwell's paintings have done more than just sell magazines. They are in large measure the visual memory of a nation.

There may be nothing especially haunting about a Rockwell painting, yet it somehow sticks with you so that today many Americans can describe several Rockwell paintings in vivid detail, even though they may not have seen the works for twenty or thirty years. Such intricate detail is a mark of Rockwell's genius: to enter a room in a Rockwell painting is to breathe familiar air. Everything is just as you remembered it. Perhaps even the faces look vaguely familiar! His realistic style helps you to accept the emotional truth of a scenario even before you absorb what is actually happening in the painting. It is a frozen moment—but one that contains such movement and vitality that the viewer searches for more. Each painting tells a story, and the clues to the narrative are in the details.

In "Breaking Home Ties," we see at first glance a young man and an older man (probably father and son) sitting on the running board of an ancient pickup. The boy looks off to the distance with welcome anticipation while

Going and Coming (1947)

his father, worn down with years of hard work and sacrifice, gazes in the other direction and absent-mindedly fingers his son's brand-new hat. The State U. sticker on his suitcase tells us that the son is off to college, possibly as the first college-bound member of his family. His carefully pressed suit and the parcel in his hands—a meal neatly packed in white paper and tied with string—bespeak of a mother back home who has already said her tearful goodbyes. The faithful dog, sensing his master's imminent departure, lays his chin upon a knee and gazes soulfully up at him. In a moment the train whistle will sound, and perhaps the anxious young man will leap to his feet and startle the dog. The father will slowly rise and squint into the sun, with a pained expression and a resignation in his weary body, and gaze one last time at his son, who is no longer a boy. Perhaps he will even embrace him before the young man climbs aboard the train with his battered suitcase—and leans, grinning, out the window, waving with all the hopeful energy within him . . . off to make his mark on the world.

Rockwell has often been censured for presenting such an idealized rendering of America, but the nostalgic attraction of his paintings speaks of more than mere sunnyside-up cultural history: he is a spokesman for the timeless enthusiasm of every age. As Americans, we seem obsessed with finding flaws and experiencing guilt over our imperfections. We are a nation of critics, impatient to fulfill even our biggest dreams. Rockwell was not a critic, but an appreciator. He saw through the dark side of human nature to the hundred acts of kindness that remind us every day of our kinship with one another. With gentle humor and warmth, he painted ordinary people being sad, joyful, embarrassed, thoughtful, compassionate, apprehensive, funny and brave; faces and situations that can put a smile of recognition on the face of even the most cynical viewer. He proved to us that despite our fatalistic fears, our motivating reality is our undying optimism. Just as the middle-aged man in "First Signs of Spring" finds uninhibited joy in the new green shoots of spring, so Rockwell allows us to rediscover common moments of humanity and a satisfaction in recollecting the past.

"People somehow get out of your work what you put into it," said Rockwell. "If you are interested in the characters that you draw, and understand them and love them, why, the person who sees your picture is bound to feel the same way."

Rockwell's enormous body of works is really a collection of visual stories, some told again and again with different characters and at different times. But no matter what the age of the picture, Rockwell creates an irresistible desire in the viewer to know what happened before and what will happen next. He invites us to join in the storytelling by reminiscing, to do some storytelling of our own. This book is a response to that invitation.

11

Girl Returning from Camp (1940)

Childhood in America

Summer Camp

Where we lived, on a farm in Indiana, girls had work to do . . . but not much recreation. In the summertime boys swam in the lake, but girls never even learned to swim. Not a girl that I knew owned a swim suit. Had we fallen from a boat, it would certainly have been quite a catastrophe!

In the fall, boys went on hunting trips, slept outdoors, and cooked over open fires, and in winter they went skating and sledding. Girls almost never enjoyed these rustic pleasures. No wonder, then, that by the age of fourteen all I wanted was to move to the city where there was something to do!

That summer, my cousin wrote from up east and convinced my parents to let me attend Girl Scout camp in upstate New York. At first I was simply excited about my imminent escape from the farm, but once I arrived at camp I found that it was much, much more. That summer, I learned to swim and dive, to build a campfire, and to paddle a canoe.

Until then, hills and trees had been merely landscape to me. Now I began to learn about wildflowers and birds, how to identify trees by their leaves and bark, and how to search for signs of wildlife nearby. We whittled and wove baskets and hammocks, built lean-tos, and slept under the stars on soft beds of pines needles. We discovered that there was more to our world than just housework and farm chores. That summer was a real rite of passage for us all, and we proved to ourselves that we could master something physical. We discovered that we were strong!

One of Uncle Sam's Assets (1921)

1956

Although I have many memories from my summers at camp, I remember the crafts projects best. There was the birdhouse made of popsicle sticks, the felt pillow with "Mom" on one side and "Dad" on the other, wallets laced with gimp, whistle lariats woven with the box stitch, pressed flowers, pine-cone dolls, copper enameled pins, beaten-copper ash trays, Indian beaded headbands, rawhide ankle bracelets, oatmeal-box tomtoms, reed baskets, lentil and pea mosaics . . . and even more!

On rainy days, especially, the crafts pavilion would be full of kids hammering, gluing, stringing beads, and either chatting away or silently concentrating on their creative processes. I never knew exactly what it was . . . whether the sound of the rain on the roof, the smell of the woods in the breeze, or the murmur of all those busy and directed children . . . but such impressions always made me feel that all was right with the world.

1963

Douglas captured the snapping turtle near the pond with a stick and a bucket. He teased the enormous, flat-shelled creature with the stick and when the turtle chomped down on it, he threw the stick into the bucket and ran hollering and hooting all the way back to our cabin.

No Swimming (1921)

Boy on High Dive (1947)

Everyone was impressed with the size and ferocity of this turtle, even Jimmy Carothers who sat mesmerized by the beady-eyed, slimy monster. I was dispatched to fetch some extra muck to throw in the bottom of the bucket so Mickey (the turtle) would feel at home. Mickey was the pride of our cabin for a couple days—but the truth is, after we stowed his bucket safely under my bed during cabin inspection, we forgot about him.

When my parents came to pick me up the following Saturday, my big sister Brenda reached under the bed to pull out my pack and encountered the bucket instead. Mickey must have been hungry, because he latched onto Brenda's finger and wouldn't let go. Brenda's always been a loud-mouth, but that day her shrieks could be heard a mile away!

People came running from everywhere to see what was the matter. The camp director tried to calm Brenda, but it was no use. It took four counselors to hold her still while they poured hot water over poor Mickey, thumped his shell with a stick, and even tried to pry his jaws open with a pen knife. Finally my mother pulled out her cigarette lighter, flicked it on and held it under his chin. After a few seconds he loosened his hold and Brenda pulled her finger, purple but intact, from the traumatized turtle's mouth.

Immediately the spotlight was on Brenda, who was iced, bandaged, soothed, and promised a trip to the department store to look at that scarab bracelet she'd wanted.

Meanwhile, Jimmy and I recaptured Mickey and gingerly carried his bucket back to the pond. As we dumped him out into the water, I felt guilty . . . not about Brenda's mishap but about how we'd treated this gentle, ugly animal. To this day I can't look at wild creatures in captivity without thinking of Mickey.

Babysitting

During the first half of the century it was taken for granted that older children took care of their younger siblings. In a society where "many hands make light work," and large families were the norm, this often meant looking after more than a few brothers and sisters!

Of course, there was always a certain ambivalence about both minding and being minded by an older brother or sister. The situation could be either a benefit or a burden to both parties.

The Babysitter (1947)

But more often that not, an essential sense of fairness won out and created mutual respect and affection that lasted a lifetime.

As for the big brother or sister, being looked up to was very satisfying; instructing a younger one in the ways of the world made one feel important and wise. On the other hand, a tag-along was a nuisance! Nonetheless, to a big brother or sister, the young one could always serve as a secretly delightful pretence to play childish and thoroughly enjoyable games without losing status with friends!

Many younger siblings preferred to be considered a nuisance if it meant they could be reluctantly included in the big kids' activities, than to have to stay at home as the baby. At least an older brother or sister expected you to behave as an equal, and was willing to let you attempt all sorts of things Mother or Dad never allowed.

No amount of money could compensate for the exasperation brought about when that cuddly, docile little bundle turned cranky, though. Babysitting could be a dream if the baby slept obediently through homework, television and snacktime . . . or it could be a nightmare!

Babysitter with Screaming Infant (1947)

19

Grandma's Doll Collection (1947)

Generation Bridge

What is it that creates that special rapport between an old person and a child? As one approaches the last years of life, it is natural to reflect upon the moments that were worth living, to look back through the years at childhood and recall in vivid detail those scenes captured forever in memory. Perhaps as parents, we were too distracted and our lives were too full of business, but now, as we watch our children's children grow up, we get a new chance to feel afresh what childhood means. We might recall a special endless summer full of simple pleasures and unending adventure, with every moment eagerly-awaited and full of possibilities.

As children grow up, struggling to make sense of the world, they often find themselves butting heads with their parents. Parental expectations and explanations don't always coincide with a child's conception of what is important. Children can distinguish right from wrong, and have a sense of fairness and idealism that is uncluttered by the complexities and compromises of adult life.

Old people can unexpectedly be a child's allies; they don't try to mediate or lecture, but simply listen as friends. Strange as it seems, after a lifetime of "facing reality," older people choose to nurture idealism. As a child discovers that life gets progressively more confusing, the patience, stability, wisdom and unconditional acceptance of an older friend is important.

Perhaps it is a matter of time . . . both children and old people have it. Time to listen, to confide, to dream, and to discover or rediscover that a true friend is a treasure, and that shared time is the best.

Cellist and Little Girl Dancing (1923) 21

Danny

I can make the bunny ears, but I can't figure out how they go together to make a bow. Mommy and Daddy are too busy to teach me to tie my shoes, but Grandpa waits patiently while I struggle with the laces. He doesn't jump in and do it for me, either. "You're doing a great job," he says, nodding his head. "It just takes practice." And I know that Grandpa will practice with me as long as I want.

Meg

Mrs. Meltzer next door is the best audience! My friend Betsy and I take our Nutcracker record over to her house, and after a plateful of ginger snaps with cream cheese, we clear the furniture and prepare for the performance. Mrs. Meltzer says, "Wait 'til I get settled, girls," and lowers herself into the flowered armchair opposite the curtained doorway. That's where Betsy and I make our entrances. It takes us a few minutes to get into our dancing skirts and fairy crowns, but when we peek out Mrs. Meltzer is always still sitting there patiently with a little smile on her face. We dance and dance to the whole Nutcracker record; Mrs. Meltzer hums along with every melody (especially "Waltz of the Flowers") and then claps her crooked hands and calls, "Bravo!" She's the best audience of all.

Arlene

As I trudge through the woods with my 4-year-old grandson, I find myself gazing through his eyes at our surroundings. We both hug a tree, and feel the rough bark against our cheeks. We examine the veins in an old dried leaf and compare it to the veins in my wrinkled hand. A cluster of toadstools becomes a gnome's secret garden; and a mossy bank becomes the king and queen's thrones—a perfect spot to sit and throw stones in the stream. All is fresh, new, fantasy. How could I ever forget how rich childhood is?

Girl at Mirror (1954)

23

Ben

I like to give a little something to my grandchildren on their birthdays, but I don't always know what they'd like. On Jessica's tenth birthday, I was stumped! Perhaps this year I would have to revert to one of those little cards with windows, where Abraham Lincoln or another green face peeks out. But I never liked sending money; it seems so impersonal. Finally, I called Jessica and asked her what she wanted for her birthday.

"I have an idea. What are you doing Tuesday afternoons?" The truth is, aside from soap operas, my afternoons are pretty clear. So are my evenings and mornings. "Gramps, why don't we learn to ice-skate together?" she said. "That's what I want for my birthday. I could meet you after school at the ice rink."

I was speechless for a moment, then reached my decision the next! "Great. I'll sign us up!"

When my daughter found out about this, she shrieked, "Honestly Dad, it's perfectly foolish. At your age . . . you might fall and break your hip, and you know what that means. . ." But Jessica had complete faith in me. Five weeks later, we held hands and glided **almost** gracefully across the ice together. What a team!

Leslie

One week before my high school graduation my mother died suddenly of a heart attack. It was as if someone had simply pushed the stop-button on my life. I was frozen, numb. Dad was devastated. The week after the funeral, he was so grief-stricken that he could hardly make himself get out of bed in the morning. I didn't have the strength to comfort him.

At first, neighbors dropped by with the requisite casseroles and condolences. But then the two of us were left alone with nothing but painful silence. That's when Mrs. Friedman arrived. She was a widow who lived down the alley from us. She brought a basket laden with flour, baking powder and yeast cakes, and in her soft voice asked whether we might like to bake bread. Together we measured, mixed, kneaded, and baked almost a dozen loaves of bread. I remember the feel of that dough as I rolled and punched it, and the wonderful smell of the crusty bread. I became so absorbed in my task that the leaden feeling began to leave my limbs. Mrs. Friedman didn't need to say a word. As the three of us stood in that warm kitchen together, I began to realize that in time the pain might finally become bearable, and someday I'd be able to say goodbye to my mother at last.

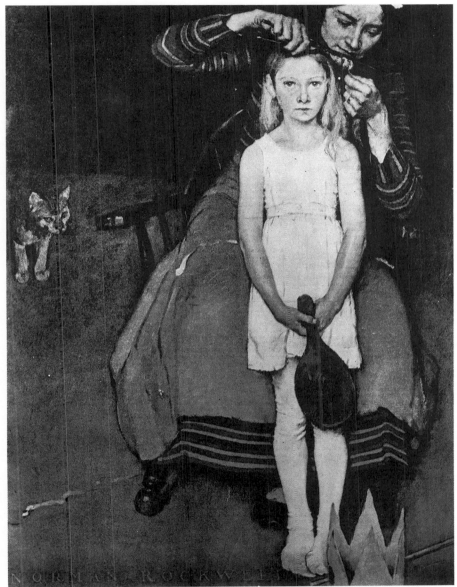

Johanna's Christmas Star (1937)

School Pageant

One of the most memorable events in childhood is participating in a school play. Since time immemorial, the best teachers have chosen plays with enough characters to allow each child a line (or at least a gesture)—

25

usually delivered in breathy haste. Costumes are a tribute to the ingenuity of parents, and traditionally test the fortitude of children in the face of discomfort for the sake of the production. In spite of the anxiety, forgotten lines, uncooperative sets and props, the pride emanating from the audience in the school auditorium is enough to float the building.

Pageant Angel (1959)

Christmas Plays

In the school Christmas pageant, there were always a certain number of plum roles. For boys, the part of Joseph or a Wise Man was top billing. Girls hoped to land Mary's part, or that of an angel. The others were animals—and heaven help the poor soul who got the part of the donkey.

Tableaux were a popular format for pageants. That way, the best reader in the class could narrate while the rest of the players had only to stand still. But this was harder than it looked! Nobody told to stand perfectly still under hot lights wearing a fake-fur beard and his father's bathrobe while the narrator intones verse after verse from the Bible will say that it's easy. "Think **statue**," suggested Mrs. Trainor. "Imagine you're made of marble, frozen forever . . . don't move a muscle!" I'd never dreamed it was possible, but I began to feel sorry for Buster Newton sweating it out under an enormous donkey-head.

"Candy" was the theme for the first-grade pageant. Everyone was either a lollipop who wore a round cardboard sandwich-sign painted in poster paints, or a candy cane who sported a red-and-white-striped flannel nightgown and an enormous, curved head-dress.

26

The "scratch, scratch, scratch" of the phonograph needle indicated that it was time to hold hands and form a circle. Then, with the first blaring note of "Santa Claus is Coming to Town," everyone skipped around trying not to trip over their nightgowns, or knock anyone over when they turned their lollipops.

Second-graders sang carols in sweetly off-key voices, or else yelled rousing renditions of "Jingle Bells" in order to make themselves heard over an enthusiastic Billy Wake who shook the sleigh bells. Mrs. Frank, the music teacher, directed the choir—her fat arms swinging vigorously as she formed a little "O" with her mouth when she wanted us to sing more quietly. A trio of recorder players who had practiced "O How a Rose" for months made a toddler in the front row burst into laughter at the first "toot, toot" from their instruments.

Other Productions

Of course, there were other plays, too. Although the boys complained bitterly about having to wear tights, we always enjoyed the dueling scenes in the play the best. No one had choreographed these scenes, and they often went on and on to the delight of everyone both in the audience and on stage. As for lines, we simply rattled them off as rapidly as they would leave our lips, with no expression. We just wanted to get through them. The star of the show was Frank Butz, who had practiced dying for a month. How convincingly he gasped and writhed on the floor! His death-throes lasted far longer that our teacher might have wished, but she realized it was the only real drama in the play. I thought Frank was magnificent!

I'll never forget one magical evening, when I was seven years old, watching a play in the school auditorium. All of a sudden the stage lights turned blue and the fairy queen floated on stage, a graceful little girl in a sparkling dress with rouge on her cheeks, waving a wand topped by a bright gold star. My mouth dropped open, my chest got tight. She was so beautiful that it almost hurt to look at her. Never before had I felt such a wave of tenderness.

As I lay in bed later that night, long after the play was over she was all I could think about. I'd close my eyes and see her perfect little face and experience that dizzy, tingling feeling all over again. It seemed as if my life would never be the same! Taking out my pen knife, I carefully carved a tiny star into the side of the maple night stand.

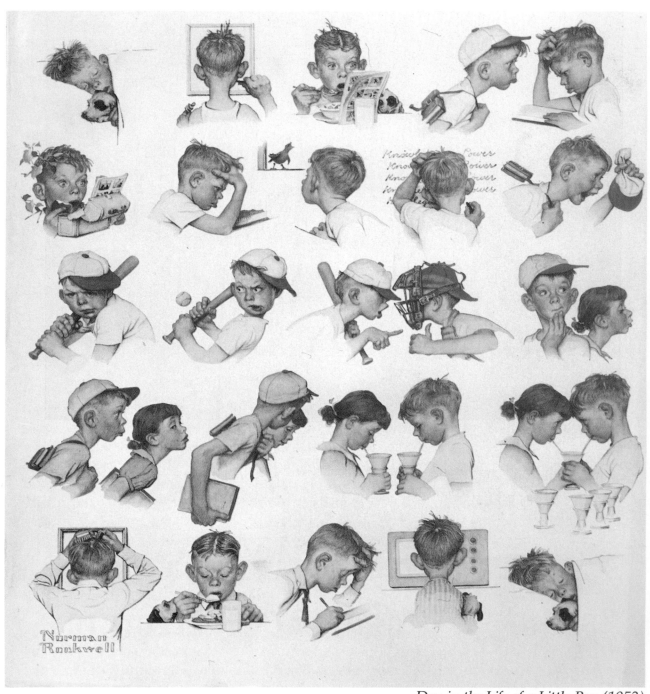

Day in the Life of a Little Boy (1952)

Todays Children

In a 1916 issue of the **Saturday Evening Post** there is an advertisement for a boy's magazine that features "everything under the sun that interests and inspires, that amazes and amuses a real boy . . . there are Indian stories by a member of the Blackfoot tribe, athletic stories, adventures of the Canadian Mounted Police, stories of business life and practice, stories of the motion picture studio, of the Army, of camping, fishing, and hunting; articles for the outdoor boy, biographies of boys who used their brains; thrilling historical articles; departments devoted to how to make money, how to get strong, how to do things, how to make things, electricity, chemistry, photography, birds, stamps, puzzles, novel inventions and natural wonders."

Are American boys—and girls—any different today? Certainly children still ask a million questions and have a burning desire to understand "grownup" things—but the more we expect children to participate in the adult world, the more it mystifies them. Childhood is a time for growing—a time to look, listen, feel and dream. The mysteries of who they will become belongs to another time. It is a remarkable phenomenon, and an act of pure faith and bravery, that a child faces the uncertainty of his future with such humor, optimism and eagerness. Perhaps, when we look at the children portrayed by Rockwell, it is that brightness in ourselves that makes us smile in recognition.

Little Girl Looking Downstairs (1964)

The Apothecary (1939)

America at Work

Druggist

Across the street from the courthouse and down three steps to the basement of the old bank building was Fraker's Drugstore. I remember the dark wood walls and black-and-white-checkered floor. It was a cool spot on a hot summer day, and well worth the half-mile walk to town.

Doc Fraker didn't stand behind a six-foot-high counter like pharmacists of today. He could be found stocking shelves, sweeping the floor or talking politics with his customers by the newspaper rack. There was sure to be lively talk when lawyers from the courthouse dropped by. Doc was interested in his "patients." He knew their medical histories, and probably their parents' and grandparents' as well.

Besides drugs and cosmetics, gauze bandages, trusses, walking canes, and crutches, Fraker's also sold other things. Every year I did my Christmas shopping at Fraker's—a new handkerchief for Father, pink writing paper for Mother, and horehound drops or licorice in a white paper sack for my brother, Howard.

But it was the back of Fraker's Drugstore that attracted every kid in town. After school a parade of book-toting children, especially high-school kids, packed the booths and counter at Fraker's soda fountain. The counter was a four-inch-thick slab of cool black marble. Gleaming chrome handles on the soda and phosphate dispensers and pyramids of shiny tin-cup holders turned upside-down made me think of a rajah's palace every time I stepped up to order my five-cent favorite, lemon phosphate. If you wanted a first sip of ambrosia, you waited until all the sweet lemon syrup sank to the bottom of the white paper cone.

In fourth grade, Harriet Lessner told a group of us on the playground that she was going to go for broke and spend the birthday money from her grandmother, the entire fifty cents, on a banana split . . . and eat the whole thing herself. Doc's part-time help, Bill Starling, was behind the counter when twelve fourth-graders marched up, led by the girl of the moment. Harriet calmly ordered her banana split and carefully laid two quarters on the black marble.

It seemed like hours in the preparation. Two bananas sliced in half, five scoops of ice cream topped alternately with chocolate sauce, nuts, whipped cream and pineapple syrup, and finally a cherry. When Bill placed the dish in front of Harriet it was as big as a turkey platter. But Harriet did not hesitate. She dug in while her audience sat or stood in awed silence, watching her every bite. Fifty cents was a lot of money—but as we watched, in our hearts we knew it was money well spent.

Shaftsbury Blacksmith Shop (1940)

Blacksmith

The horseshoe-forging contest reflects what Americans still believe is essential to a winning economy—hard work, the best personal effort by all workers, competition in a free market, and guaranteed vocational training for all those who want to learn a skill. But as recently as sixty years ago, there was another primary source of energy essential to our economy—the horse.

All the services provided by a town or city were powered by the horse. Horse-drawn trolleys were the major form of transportation. Produce from farms reached city markets by horse-drawn wagons. Delivery of milk and bread, garbage collection and laundry services all depended on horses and wagons. Even fire protection depended on horse-drawn fire trucks. Farmers used horses to pull plows and reapers. For the military it was the horse that pulled artillery and supplies and made the cavalry possible.

Maintenance of this invaluable energy source made the blacksmith's skill a necessity in every town across America. The local blacksmith's shop was often no more than a roof over a forge, where a leather-aproned man manufactured iron shoes, tools, wagon wheel rims and the like.

Many times the blacksmith was also a farrier, fitting and shoeing the horses as well. First the old horseshoe was removed and the hooves trimmed or pared down. Then a shoe similar in size was selected. The blacksmith/farrier placed it in the fire and, using bellows, heated up the fire until the iron shoe became so hot that it glowed red and softened. Taking the shoe from the fire with tongs, the blacksmith hammered the shoe on an anvil, shaping it to fit the horse's hoof. When the shoe was cool, the farrier hammered nails through the bottom of the horse's hoof so that they poked out the side. These edges were filed down and the horse was shod.

Horse owners truly appreciated a good blacksmith/farrier. If a horse's shoes did not fit properly, it could damage the horse for life. By working with horses, many blacksmiths were damaged for life, too. In addition to burns and eye damage from flying sparks, kicks and bites from uncooperative horses were occupational hazards that often resulted in cracked ribs, broken legs and toes, and even death. But the blacksmith was an indispensible part of every community, and the caretaker of the undisputed power source of the nation.

Farmer and Bird (1923)

Farmer

In 1923 most farms were small. The amount of land one family could cultivate with a horse-drawn plow limited the size and productivity of the farm. Then as now, farming was a lot of hard work with no vacations. Farmers were completely at the mercy of the weather. Drought, storms, and insects could ruin a family in one season.

This aspect of farming has not changed. It is still a risky way of life. But agricultural methods have changed drastically and have changed the way farmers live today. The agricultural methods used by the farmers of the Midwest to break the sod of the plains eventually led to the great Dustbowl of 1934 and a mass exodus from the rural life to city dwelling. This migration from country to city continues today. The number of farmers in the U.S. is still dwindling as small farms are swallowed up into larger and larger tracts. Yet with fewer farms and farmers, productivity has greatly increased.

While Rockwell's strong but gentle farmer mowed his fields by hand with a scythe, working to put food on the table for his family, today's farmer runs his farm like a corporation. A revolution in farming methods has occurred that, by the 1950s, could already be called "agribusiness." Mechanization, electrification, use of fertilizers and pesticides, and better management increased the size of farms. It also increased their productivity. Now, the American farmer's problem is food surpluses. More and more American grain is finding its way to hungry people around the globe. As one Future Farmer of America put it, "I want to be a farmer because I think it is the most important job there is. What could be more important than feeding the world?"

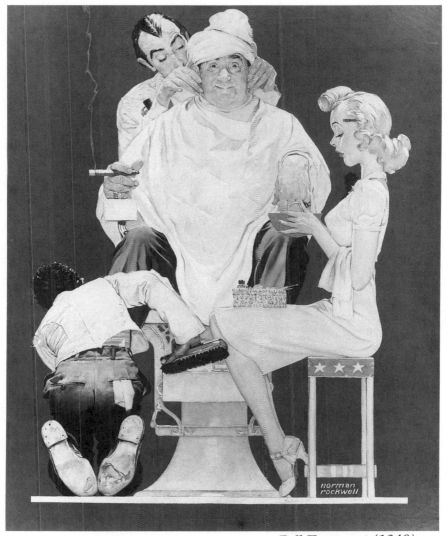

Full Treatment (1940)

Barber

Walter anticipated a high-class evening with Shirley. The hotel's Palm Room featured a dance band that was really smooth. Shirley would wear her sharp blue dress and she'd look just like Ginger Rogers. He would be Fred Astaire—debonair, sophisticated. He wanted more than just a shave and a haircut. He needed to shine from his fingertips to the tips of his tap-tapping shoes. Fortunately, the hotel barbershop employed barbers, manicurists, and shoe-shine boys.

Walter would not have found the same services at regular barbershops throughout America. Most barbers did not work in such luxurious surroundings. The town barbershop was more like a local hangout or club-house for regular customers. Often above the mirrors hung a shelf lined with private shaving mugs, each marked with the name of a patron. Men dropped in at the barbershop to read racy magazines like the **Police Gazette**, to place a bet on a horse, or to enjoy an argument about politics or sports and, of course, to get a shave and a haircut.

Once his customer was in the chair, the barber would ask, if he didn't already know, "Spoon or thumb?" The barber could use either to stretch the skin on the cheek for a close shave. A barber needed to be a skilled conversationalist or a great listener because clip-and-talk, snip-and-talk was the barber way. The men-only atmosphere allowed customers to relax and exercise more freedom in their exclamations than when ladies were present. And ladies were rarely, if ever, present. The only time a woman set foot in a barbershop was to deposit or collect small boys.

Women at Work

Before World War II, it was considered improper for married women to work outside the home. After the joblessness of the Great Depression, women were especially discouraged from seeking any work position that might be occupied by a man. Women worked for pin money, men to support their families. But when the work force was shipped across the oceans to fight the Germans and the Japanese, attitudes had to change.

An appeal to patriotic women to come to the aid of their country resulted in 3.5 million women working in ammunition and airplane factories. WAVEs, WACs and SPARs worked as truck drivers, airplane mechanics, typists and clerks, cooks and nurses. Many other women worked in civilian-related jobs as taxi-drivers, farmers, shopkeepers, night watchmen, bakers, technicians, and draftswomen. Employers who considered women eligible for 29 percent of the jobs available changed that figure to 55 percent after seven months of war. Daycare centers were built as a war-related expense. Vocational training for women was taken seriously for the first time. The mobilization of women was one of the greatest weapons the Allied forces had. Continuously high production of war material from America was the determining factor in the defeat of the Nazis and Japanese.

Liberty Girl (1943)

Newspaper Editor

The office of the **Munroe County Appeal,** a weekly newspaper in Paris, Missouri, is a busy place on this afternoon before press day. Editor Jack Blanton and his staff publish a newspaper that they believe is a reflection of the concerns and values of this rural community. In addition to being the only printed source of local news, **The Appeal** carries editorials, feature stories, works by a local poetess, and a livestock column. Those who wish to place classifieds before this week's deadline are lined up at the front desk.

Copy is set either on a noisy linotype machine or by hand—backwards, of course. After an edition has gone to press, the type is melted down to be used for the next edition. The weekly work cycle repeats itself year after year; the tasks are always the same, yet the news and the stories are always different, especially in the war years.

On the wall behind the front desk, below the picture of the soldier, is a gold star. It speaks of a loss. Bereaved families hung these in their win-

Norman Rockwell Visits a Country Editor (1946)

dows to let others know that their son, brother, father, or husband had been killed in action. It was a symbol of grief, of sacrifice, and of pride. During the dark days of the war in 1943-44, in church vestibules throughout America, a list of congregation members serving in the armed forces was posted. Each week a gold star was pasted next to the names of those who had been killed. On Sunday mornings anxious friends lingered in the vestibule, scanning the list.

During the war years **The Appeal** was also a bearer of ill tidings. While life seemed to go by each week as usual, with livestock, weather reports and local news, events on the other side of the world were deeply affecting the lives of people in Paris, Missouri. Jack Blanton felt that his job was to report those events and try to make some sense out of them.

Statue of Liberty

Independence Day, 1946. World War II is over! The dizzying celebrations of victory are behind us and now we look ahead to an uncertain future with a possible collapse of the stimulated war economy, and a return to the Depression days—or worse. We've come out from under a terrible cloud. The world lost forty million soldiers and civilians during the war. Europe lies in ruins. By geographical luck the U.S. is unscathed and is emerging, along with the U.S.S.R., as a superpower; both countries are drawing new lines of influence on the globe. More than anything, Americans crave lasting peace. But as the Nation With The Atomic Bomb, in a rapidly changing political scene, the U.S. has new responsibilities. Americans have seen how fragile the security of liberty is. The work of the next decade, and indeed the next century, will be to keep the Lady's lamp burning.

Statue of Liberty (1946)   39

Crestwood Commuter Station (1949)

Commuters

Suburbs like Crestwood, with its nostalgic, Tudor-style houses and farmland surroundings, are clearly the old suburbs of pre-Depression times. When railroads and trolley lines extended into the country, the great escape from city crowds and grime to a semblance of rural life became possible.

After World War II, a new type of suburban life changed forever the landscape and the way we live. Vast tracts of land were bulldozed flat, and row upon row of nearly identical houses were built. These developments boasted the "best house in the U.S." and a "new way of life." For young growing families it was an answer to the basic American dream of homeownership—a snug little house with a little lawn around it, a hammock in the back yard, and maybe even a barbecue for family cookouts.

Other developers capitalized on the success of these developments and built suburbs that sprang up outside New York, Chicago, Los Angeles, and every other major city. For the non-city dweller, this meant that a daily trip by train separated his home and work life. Fellow commuters may have had much in common at home but, once on the train, a sense of commuter community was rarely established. Travel time was for solitary activities such as reading the newspaper or flipping through one's briefcase reviewing the day's work. In many cities where cars were the only

40

commuter choice, the vehicle made isolation complete. Now, inching along in bumper-to bumper traffic, a commuter could be in the midst of a crowd, yet be totally alone.

Teacher

I remember the smell of school, of the oiled wood floors. Each day Mr. Warfield, the grumpy janitor, sprinkled them with a fine, green sawdust then swept them clean. The smell of that oil mixed with the odors of homemade lunches of tomato soup and egg-salad sandwiches will always remind me of our classroom with the tall windows and the view that stretched over the ballfield to the horizon.

Because I was quite tall for my age, I was often selected to open the top windows for a little fresh air. This was a special honor because the window opener was long pole with a hook at the end. The whole class would watch intently as I raised my lance, balanced just right on my forearm, and carefully caught the ring on the top window and yanked it open with a flourish. The eyes of my classmates told me that I sat down to silent applause and cheers.

Another pole job entailed pulling down the long blackout shades to darken the room for film strips. On a warm afternoon it was inevitable that half the class would be sawing wood, heads on their desks before "The Story of Teeth" was over and the blackout shades raised again.

My third-grade teacher's name was Mrs. MacArthur. She was an enormous woman with broad shoulders and a booming voice that could cut through the loudest classroom chatter and bring us to attentive silence. We were all so eager to please that "Sit up straight and tall with your pencils on your desks" caused many to assume a ramrod straight posture that made us finally shake with the strain.

When Mrs. MacArthur laughed, those tall windows rattled. She made it easy to laugh. That woman with the presence of a mountain liked each and every one of us. The boys and girls in her class were special, destined for great things. She saw our strengths and outlined our futures—Leonard was the scientist, Becky was an artist, Dennis was a great arbiter on the playground and would be a lawyer. But with all the talk of what we would be **some** day, she was always clear about what was expected of us now. We should be direct, honest and fair with each other, just as she was with us.

Cave of the Winds (1920)

America
at Play

The Age of Play

For the first time in the 1920s, Americans actively looked for ways to spend their leisure time. The work week had been shortened from 60 to 48 hours, and a higher standard of living meant that people had more time and more money to spend. Old rural entertainments such as handicrafts and church socials did not satisfy the workers in the cities. There was a desperate need to escape from tedious factory and office work. Society began to realize that all work and no play could make Johnny sick, less productive, and a poor provider. People recognized recreation as the healthful answer. "Idle hands are the devil's playground" took on new meaning, for it seemed that people approached their newfound leisure with a strong desire to "do something." A whole population was determined to enjoy its time away from work—Americans wanted to have fun.

Sports, games, movies, radio, popular magazines, amusement parks, theater, bowling alleys, and dance halls all boomed during this period. Participation in recreation of all kinds was now open to women and they took full advantage of it. Whether it was a game of Mahjongg, learning to play a musical instrument, swimming, bowling, or listening to the radio, American men and women realized what children had known all along—that play was important.

Amusement Parks

It was 1893 at the Chicago World's Fair. Crowds of people stood in line to experience "the thrill of a lifetime." They stepped with pounding hearts into the glass cabs suspended from the girders. But once the mighty 250-foot wheel began to turn, they forgot their fear in the delightful sensation of climbing and descending, and the unforgettable view of the fair grounds. This wonderful invention opened a whole new world of family entertainment. With the success of the ferris wheel, it wasn't long before other mechanical rides were developed and the idea of the amusement park was born.

The Funny Mirror (1921)

Coney Island probably epitomizes the amusement park of the Twenties. It was a popular place for a family outing, and only a nickel-ride away at the end of the subway line. A broad, sandy beach offered an ideal place to lie in the sun and maybe splash in the water, but it was the rides, games, and food that drew both young and old to the park. The first stop was the enormous merry-go-round, for a dizzying whirl on the horses and other creatures, where even the littlest had a seat or a saddle. Next door was Nathan's, famous for its foot-long hot dogs. At Coney Island, food lovers could find steamed clams, corn on the cob, ice cream, cotton candy—all they needed for fortification to face the thrills and chills of the day. There were bumper cars, a haunted house, the tunnel of love (a boat ride in the dark). . . but the biggest thrill, and a ride only for those with the strongest constitutions, was the most hair-raising of all. It was advertised as the fastest and most dangerous roller coaster in the world—the Cyclone!

When the tests of nerves were over, fun-seekers could turn to the tests of strength and skill. Along the boardwalk, hopefuls tried to knock wooden milk bottles over with one pitch, hit the duck in the shooting gallery, or swing the hammer hard enough to ring the bell. In the funhouse, distortion mirrors sent viewers into gales of laughter, as did the "cave of winds" where jets of air blew up from the floor to startle those who stepped over them. Concealed nearby was the jet operator who watched through a crack to see when pretty girls or fat ladies walked over the grating, then released the breeze.

Crossword Puzzles

One year before this cover painting was produced, a new publishing company released 3,600 copies of its first book. Booksellers expressed doubts about whether it would ever sell. Their biggest order came from a bookstore buyer who took twenty-five copies out of friendship for the publishers, hoping he could sell a few.

But everyone had underestimated the whims of the American public. The book was called **The Crossword-Puzzle Book** and within months of its publication (and three subsequent editions), three-quarters of a million copies had been sold. The crossword-puzzle craze was born. Other publishers quickly followed suit and published puzzle books for children, Bible crossword books, "celebrity" crosswords devised by famous people, and ethnic crosswords galore. The sales of dictionaries and thesauruses skyrocketed. Solving puzzles was such a popular pastime that B&O put

The Crossword Puzzle (1925)

dictionaries in all the trains on its main line.

In New York, a man was jailed for refusing to leave a restaurant after hours of trying to solve a crossword puzzle. A minister from Pittsburgh inserted the text of his sermon into a puzzle. Couples spent evenings together poring over the dictionary and asking, "What's a two-letter word for Egyptian sun god?"

By the end of 1925, the fad had faded. Although crosswords are still published by newspapers and enjoyed by many, crossword-puzzle mania, like trivia madness in the '80s, peaked and then quickly lost popular attention.

Toys

There was a time when nearly all toys were child-powered (or in this case, grandfather-powered). Favorite toys brought by Santa to little boys included Erector sets, Lincoln logs, baseball gloves and bats, lead soldiers, cast metal trucks and cars, bikes, sleds, and clasp knives (these were included with a new pair of hiking shoes that featured a pocket on the side for carrying the knife). Of course, exceptions to the child-powered standbys were such items as electric-powered trains and wind-up mechanical toys such as the monkey clapping the cymbals and mass-produced tin fire trucks, motorcycles, and circus figures. Children made many of their own toys, too. Kites, whirligigs, puppets, toy boats, bubble pipes, and slingshots were part of the childhood of most boys who grew up in the Twenties and Thirties.

It was in the Thirties that cereal companies and others realized that children could influence the buying habits of a family. They introduced the "free toy with proof-of-purchase coupons" on the labels of their products and exploited the popularity of fantasy heroes. Here whistle and code rings, special badges, pocket knives, water pistols, watches, and yoyos initiated children into a secret and exciting world that was really, after all powered by their imaginations.

Grandfather and Boy on Rocking Horse (1933)   47

Golf

The game of golf was introduced in the 1890s and was initially played by well-to-do people at private golf courses. But it gained popularity so rapidly that by 1924 there were two million golfers and 184 municipal golf links in the United States. With the decline of the private golfing club during the Depression, the number of municipal golf links rose to 576 within the next ten years. There was clearly a democratization of the sport and of other "gentlemanly sports" as well. As a result, middle-class as well as working-class people became avid golfers, swimmers, skiers, and played soccer, rugby, squash, and tennis.

Man Leaving Work to Go Golfing (1919)

Then, in 1930, there was a development that brought the game of golf to every man, woman, and child in America: miniature golf courses sprouted up on vacant lots from coast to coast, and another American craze was born. The design of the miniature or pee-wee golf course incorporated elaborate and zany motifs to enhance its tunnels, drawbridges, slopes, and mazes. Jungles, castles, miniature Taj Mahals, windmills, and pirate ships created an atmosphere of fantasy and an escape from reality that families of the Depression sorely needed. The widespread fad was short-lived, but resurfaced again in the 1950s. At that time, interest in golf saw a national resurgence when the country witnessed President Eisenhower's passion for the game. In fact it was rare to see the President pictured without a golf club in his hand! Golf courses again sprang up, this time in the newly-built suburbs where a Saturday morning game of golf was such a common pastime that it became a cliche'.

Radio

The first radio my family owned was a crystal set built by my father in 1922. I remember him carefully winding the three coils that were to serve as the tuner. By sliding them back and forth, I could tune in orchestra broadcasts from New York through the earphones.

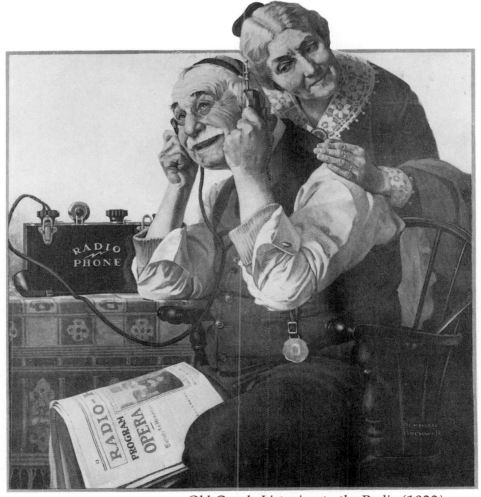

Old Couple Listening to the Radio (1922)

Four years later we bought the Cadillac of radios, for $50. We purchased it on time, taking a year to pay it off. It looked like a long, gold-colored tool box with a separate round speaker that sat on top. That same year our neighbors, the Webers, bought a beautiful radio that was really a piece of furniture, a massive square wood cabinet with a big gold tuning dial. Mrs. Weber enjoyed the daytime soap operas, and sat captivated by the eternal question: Could a girl from a small mining town in the West find happiness as the wife of a wealthy and titled Englishman?

The programs my brothers and I listened to were adventure tales. My sister liked storytelling programs, especially the one with the lady who told fairy tales in the sweetest voice you ever heard. Another popular show at my house was an amateur hour. I remember the time the show featured a man who played the spoons. Before he began, the announcer asked the man his occupation. When the man said he was a garbage man, the audience laughed. The announcer then lectured the audience on the value of honest labor. After a moment of silence there was a spontaneous burst of applause.

In those Depression days it seemed the whole city stopped at seven o'clock each evening and sat in front of their radios. Whenever I think about those radios days, I think of theme songs and advertising jingles. The sponsors and shows are somehow inextricably paired in my head— just as the advertisers probably intended.

My father's favorite radio personality was a sportscaster—although he couldn't get enough comedy shows, either. On Friday nights, Mr. Weber would invite my father over to listen to the fights.

Every year my mother, who had been born and raised in England, stayed up late to listen to the King's New Year's Day address. It always sounded very crackly and far away, with occasional whooshing sounds. I was sure this was the sound of the waves crashing against the underwater cable.

Much more clearly audible, of course, were the President's fireside chats. It was the first time a president talked to us regularly in our homes. Radio must have been a blessing for Roosevelt, who couldn't travel much. It gave him a way to sidestep an unwilling Congress and lay his plans directly before the American public.

In 1938, the airwaves became the scene of a Halloween hoax that upset many people, or at least embarrassed them: Martians were to invade planet Earth. Some people thought it was a real invasion from Mars; they panicked, packed up their families, and were ready to leave the city. Of course, no one in my neighborhood admitted to having been fooled!

One tragic broadcast in 1937 has stuck with me through the years: it was a routine broadcast from Lakehurst, New Jersey, describing the docking of a zeppelin called the Hindenberg. It suddenly burst into flames at its moorings. The announcer tried to continue describing the horror of the scene, but the loss of life so overwhelmed him that he broke down and began to cry.

There were so many shows I can recall, you'd think that all we did in those days was listen to the radio. Radio somehow helped us through the Depression. It wasn't so much the escapism, but rather the way in which it pointed out our common humanity again and again.

Bridge Game (1948)

Contract Bridge

The year 1930 stands as the golden year for the game of contract bridge. Although it had been played as an after-dinner amusement by the upper class for some time, average Americans did not discover it until that year. Suddenly, while other manufacturing businesses were collapsing, playing card manufacturers were enjoying the best sales figures they'd ever had. Books on bridge become overnight bestsellers. Newspapers and radio reported on contract bridge games played in fancy hotels while readers and listeners noted each play and critiqued the games with their friends. Children learned to play bridge, and it became a family affair—even eclipsing for a time the popularity of pinochle and poker among male card players.

Although interest in the game faded during World War II, the middle class of post-war America rediscovered the card party and formed bridge clubs. Bridge brought women of the suburbs together regularly. It was a comforting ritual that reminded many isolated homemakers that they were not alone. Couples enjoyed the friendly competition and the chance to gather around the card table once a week and socialize. In a lifestyle where work, home maintenance, and scheduled leisure were the rule, "bridge night" was a reason to make time for good friends.

Television

When television was demonstrated at the New York World's Fair in 1939, most people considered it a complicated toy with limited possibilities. An underground cable stretched from the RCA Building to the Empire State Building, and from there up to a transmitter mounted upon the top of the skyscraper. There were only perhaps two hundred television sets in existence and they were all owned by people who lived very close to the transmitter and thus were within broadcast range. Programming included travelogues, one-act plays, newsreels and whatever else could be produced cheaply. Movie stars and well-known actors certainly could not be paid on what little advertising revenue the new medium attracted.

But the novelty of television did find a place in the cocktail lounge. Barkeepers discovered that television was a cheaper attraction than live entertainment. It wasn't long, however, before their patrons wanted sets in their own homes. Additional transmitters were built—and with more experience and sponsorship money, television programming became more appealing by featuring sports events, fashion shows, plays, and feature films; even well-known radio voices made the transition from sound alone to image on the television screen.

New Television Antenna (1949)

The first television in the neighborhood was a huge wooden cabinet with a tiny rounded screen, yet every child within miles, it seemed, was only too happy to gather around its glow to watch the magic screen. Other families would follow suit and purchase a console set for between $150 and $400.

In the early years, most television programming was live. The biggest star was "Mr. Television" himself, whose kooky show won the hearts of the American people by virtue of its outrageous zaniness. First-class live drama entered the homes of viewers who otherwise would never have seen New York stage productions. By the 1950s, teleplays became television classics and symbols of television's golden age. It was observed that more people watched "Hamlet" on the night in 1953 when it was broadcast, than had seen the play in all its performances since its first staging more than 350 years before.

In 1949, Americans bought 100,000 television sets a week. Old radio favorites successfully made the transition to the screen, and were joined by popular heroes. Sports, news, game shows, talk shows, and sitcoms were all developed in those first early days of television.

Television's impact upon American politics, self-image, family life, children, buying habits, values, crime, and world views is still being assessed. There is no question that 1939's "complicated toy" has affected the American people.

Leisure Fashion

Fashion-setters of today would be shocked at the apparel people at the turn of the century wore to participate in sports. Long heavy skirts that inhibited free movement caused some of the best women tennis players of the day to lose matches. Bathing suits for men and women were certainly not designed for swimming. Golf had its own uniform but it was heavy, cumbersome, and not appropriate for swinging the club. For the middle classes, work clothes and play clothes were the same thing—formal.

Then came the Twenties, and everything changed. Women set fashion trends that shortened and lightened skirts, dropped waists, and allowed for the movement necessary to dance the Charleston. Men's fashions also loosened up. Eventually clothing manufacturers found a market for "leisure wear." In the Twenties this might have meant elegant lounging paja-

The Swimming Hole (1945) 55

mas for around the house, but by the Thirties, women were wearing loose-fitting slacks to do the gardening, "playsuits," shorts, short tennis skirts, and beach pajamas. Men were wearing bright colors. By the 1940s the sporty, tanned look was becoming popular.

Leisure wear aside, this salesman has hung up his work clothes, a well-worn summer suit with saddle shoes, and escapes even leisure wear by swimming in the most appropriate fashion—his birthday suit.

Bicycling

Since the invention of the "safety bicycle" and the pneumatic tire in 1888, the bicycle has been extremely popular in Europe. The same has not been true in America. Although Americans never really established a love affair with bicycles, during the Depression we took great interest in the six-day bicycle race. Perhaps it was European-born fans that started the interest, but newspapers and radio made the bicycle race a national event. For six days bicyclists rode around and around, eating ten small meals per day and stopping only for short naps and muscle massages. It held the same appeal as marathon dancing—endurance was what one admired. But as much as Americans enjoyed the race, it did not cause an upsurge in bicycle riding.

Children in the United Stated have enjoyed bike riding for many years. But somehow, when they grew up, bicycles were put aside with other toys. Not until our present health-conscious era have adults rediscovered the joys of self-propulsion and the pleasure of sightseeing in the open air.

Springtime in Stockbridge (1971)

Boy Painting Girl's Slicker (1927)

Romance in America

Puppy Love

He was my sweetheart and my best friend for years, but by fourth grade we had grown apart. What began as a kindergarten romance ended in an argument on the ballfield when I slid into second and he pronounced me out (I was safe by a mile). Things were never the same after that.

Bobbie Black was shy in kindergarten. In fact he never spoke to anyone but me. The teacher was a bit worried about that. She finally called in our respective parents to see if they wanted to separate Bobbie and me. Fortunately, good sense prevailed and we remained together. I smothered Bobbie—cornering him in the cloakroom for a kiss, following him home from school every day. He had a big family, and I loved to sit in the kitchen with his mother, a beautiful woman, and chat while Bobbie played ball with his brothers in the back yard and other siblings wandered in and out.

Mrs. Black was the kindest and most sensible woman I ever knew. When I dreamed about growing up, getting married, and having children, it was always her life I anticipated. I would be blond, capable and gentle, binding my household together merely by my presence. And of course, Bobbie would be my husband.

Each Valentine's Day I'd save my money to buy Bobbie a valentine the size of Michigan. Like a true best friend, he was never embarrassed when it wouldn't fit into the slot of the big cardboard box and instead sat propped up next to it with "Bobbie" covered with lipstick kisses, made with my mother's "passionflame red."

But we drifted apart, and eventually Bobbie moved away. I heard that he was a great basketball player in college, and then became a doctor. A few years ago, Bobbie came to town and we got together again for a bittersweet evening. We pored over old scrapbooks and laughed until we cried. He remembered every detail of those sweetheart days, even down to the way I used to tuck in his scarf for him each day before recess. He admitted that Valentine's Day has never really been the same since.

Boy and Girl Gazing at Moon (1926)

No Credit Given (1917)

Lost Love

She had dark-brown curly hair that fell below her shoulders and the longest eyelashes I had ever seen. She wore shiny pink ribbons and soft blue sweater vests. I'd been watching Eve since school started that September and actually spoke to her twice without making a fool of myself. Now as the Christmas holidays approached I had worked up enough courage to ask her for her picture. I'm sure my Adam's apple danced a lot in my scrawny neck as I took the wallet-sized photo from her warm hand.

That holiday, George, who went to a private boarding school upstate, came to stay with us. We'd hardly picked him up at the train station before I was showing him Eve's picture.

"Great-looking girl," said George. "When do I get to see her in person?"

"We're invited to a Christmas party at her house on Saturday," I told him. George smiled—an amazingly confident smile for a fourteen-year-old. And then I began to feel a little uneasy.

As Eve opened the door that Saturday the warm glow of the Christmas lights were like a halo about her head. She looked so serene and sweet that I just stood and gazed at her for a moment. George saw no reason for hesitation. He flashed his famous smile and before I knew what was happening he was already following Eve through the living room, and being ceremoniously introduced to her father. After the requisite handshakes and my own weak "hello," I followed George and Eve down to the club-basement decorated with tinsel and lights. I remember leaning against the knotty pine paneling at the foot of the stairs and watching George scoop a drink from the punch bowl and hand it to Eve. Their eyes met and my heart sank.

Throughout the rest of the party, I sat with the rest of the fellows on cold metal folding-chairs stuffing my face with sugar cookies, just watching. I was numb. On the way home, George upbraided me for not being more aggressive.

"I had to do all the talking," he said. "Why didn't you ask her to dance or get her a drink? You can't just sit there with the nerds and expect her to like you. I can see you're going to need a lot of help with this one."

The next day was cold and windy. As I sat in the kitchen staring out the window and wondering what Eve was doing, George had an idea.

"Let's get out the shovels and go over to Eve's house. We can scrape the ice off her front steps—and maybe if we hang around long enough, her mother will invite us in."

Two eager young men marched down the street and attacked the ice with a vengeance. As I chipped away, the bitter wind cutting into my face, I imagined I was clearing the way for Eve. I made certain that there was no icy spot where she might slip. I would protect her—and maybe if she came out right now and did slip, I would be there to catch her and hold her in my arms, and . . . The door opened and Eve's father poked his head out. "Come on in, boys, before you turn into popsicles!"

George dropped his shovel and sprinted up the stairs. I stood the shovels next to the house and followed him in. After the glare of the snow, it took a moment for my eyes to adjust to the dimly-lit living room but soon I saw the couch with the big roses all over, and there sat Eve. . . and already seated next to her was George. He rubbed his hands and helped himself to the hot chocolate and cookies on the coffee table. Eve watched his every move with fascination, and giggled at everything he said. I sat in the recliner, silently rocking. Like the ice on my boots, I felt myself melting too, becoming smaller and smaller until I was merely a puddle evaporating in George's sun.

When George went back to school, he and Eve wrote letters to each other. I think that's what pained me most: imagining that he held those square white notecards with the big "E" on the front and saw her own curling script spelling "Dear George. . . " it was hard to take. But I forgave him in the end.

Boy Gazing at Pictures of Stars (1934)

Girl Crazy

When was it that cowboys lost their appeal and pictures of glamourous movie stars took their places among the school pennants on the walls of my bedroom? I suppose it all began as simple curiosity about girls. For years they had been boring and beneath notice—but then indifference and disgust gave way to vague fascination, and afternoons were spent playing basketball with the guys and talking about girls. We were certain that girls were totally different creatures. They didn't think, act or smell like boys. We had a million questions . . . and could only guess at the answers.

By the time I was fifteen, my fascination had turned into an obsession. I wasn't content to play ball with the guys anymore; now I wanted to walk home with Rita, to sit next to Nancy, or to hold the water-fountain button down for my English teacher, Miss Jacobs. I even wanted to beat the erasers for Miss Dixon. Every waking moment I wanted to be near girls. Maybe this was an illness, I thought. There certainly were physical symptoms—flushed cheeks, sweaty palms, dry mouth, a rolling feeling in my stomach, dizziness—all the symptoms of terror.

"You seem a little nervous today, Mike," Miss Dixon would comment. If she only knew!

Girl Reading the Post (1941)

Starstruck

From the moment I opened my eyes in the morning, I imagined that the invisible camera was on me. I floated out of bed, just so, as gracefully as a swan-necked stage star. I brushed my hair and flung it back with a dramatic toss, just as I'd seen in the movies. At the breakfast table, I was as witty and urbane as the stars in my favorite films. As I walked to school I strolled along seductively. The invisible camera followed me everywhere.

And who was watching? Perhaps a rugged adventure hero, or that dreamy leading man. It didn't matter. So long as I was "on camera," I wasn't the slightly chubby Alice Begusky of Springfield, Illinois. I was extraordinary. I was a star!

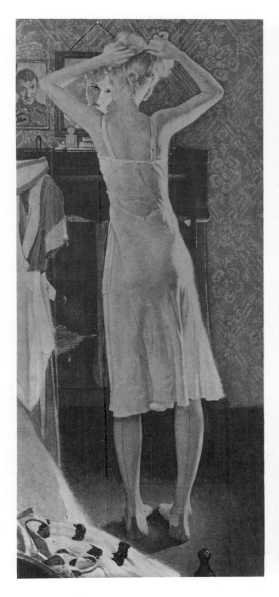 

Before the Date (1949) 65

I'll Follow You to the Ends of the Earth

The weekend was surrounded by historical events—astronauts walked on the moon, hundreds of thousands of people gathered at Woodstock, and it was also the weekend that heart-throb Wayne Decker invited me to go backpacking with him. Wayne was brilliant. He was a medical student, and I thought he must surely know all about the great outdoors and survival in the wilderness.

"You should have a good frame and backpack," he suggested. "I'll bring the sterno stove, the freeze-dried food, my Swiss Army knife and the axe. You carry the trail mix, canteen, utensils and your sleeping bag. I'll bring the tent. Oh, and don't forget to wear hiking boots and bring a poncho."

My pack weighed in at 40 pounds by the time I had assembled all the essentials for the weekend. I'm sure Wayne's was heavier. It was a hot, dry summer morning as I parked the car by a sign that read "Devil's Hole." Wayne explained that it was a short hike, only two or three miles down to the lake where we would rendezvous with some friends and make camp for the night.

"All we have to do," said Wayne, his brilliant medical hands encompassing the landscape with one sweep, "is follow the trail signs, and we'll be swimming in that cool lake before you know it." He tossed the heavy pack onto his brilliant back, I heaved up my own, and off we marched into the forest.

"There! Look at that white blaze on the tree. That marks the trail," he said knowingly. Did I say he was brilliant? I would have followed him anywhere.

As we followed the white blazes for over four hours, up and down the rocky slopes, I should have been miserable. But just watching his forearms ripple and the sweat sliding past his temples as he hacked away at the underbrush was enough for me. What had even resembled trail had long since disappeared. By late afternoon, when we were still stumbling from one white treeblaze to another, a vague shadow of doubt began to cloud my faith in Wayne. Another cloud covered the sun, and it rained cats and dogs as we sat huddled beneath my poncho, water rushing down the hillside and over my brand new and now painful hiking boots.

norman rockwell

University Club (1960)

Wayne was puzzled. Neither of us wanted to admit that we were lost, but we couldn't escape the obvious. What might have been a romantic interlude in the rain became a discussion of the incompetence of the park service, the inconvenient disappearance of the sun just when we needed it to determine which way was west, and of how Boy Scout equipment was far superior to the junk they make today. While Wayne went on and on with other brilliant observations, I speculated that perhaps the water running downhill might collect in something like a lake, and suggested that we follow it downhill.

Near the bottom of the hill we discovered a stream. Now Wayne was really excited. "All we have to do," he said, "is follow the stream to the lake!"

By now, it was getting dark. The stream finally led us to a pasture and an abandoned farm house. Nearby stood a trailer with lights on inside. Wayne knocked on the door, and we introduced ourselves to a sweet but taciturn old couple who took us in, soggy camping equipment and all, and let us spend the night.

The next morning the old man took us to our car. It was a short walk as it turned out, just over the hill. "I can't understand it," said brilliant Wayne. "We followed the white trailblazes."

"You talkin' about those white marks on the trees, son?" said the man. "Those ain't trail markers. Those mark the trees the forestry service is gonna harvest. No, no. You want to follow those big brown plaques that say 'Lake Burke' with the big white arrows pointin' down the hill."

I was just about to dissolve into gales of laughter when I thought about poor Wayne. I glanced at him, and realized he was even more appealing than he had been during his brilliant moments.

It took a long time—but now, looking back upon that weekend, he's finally beginning to see the humor in it.

The Marriage License (1955)

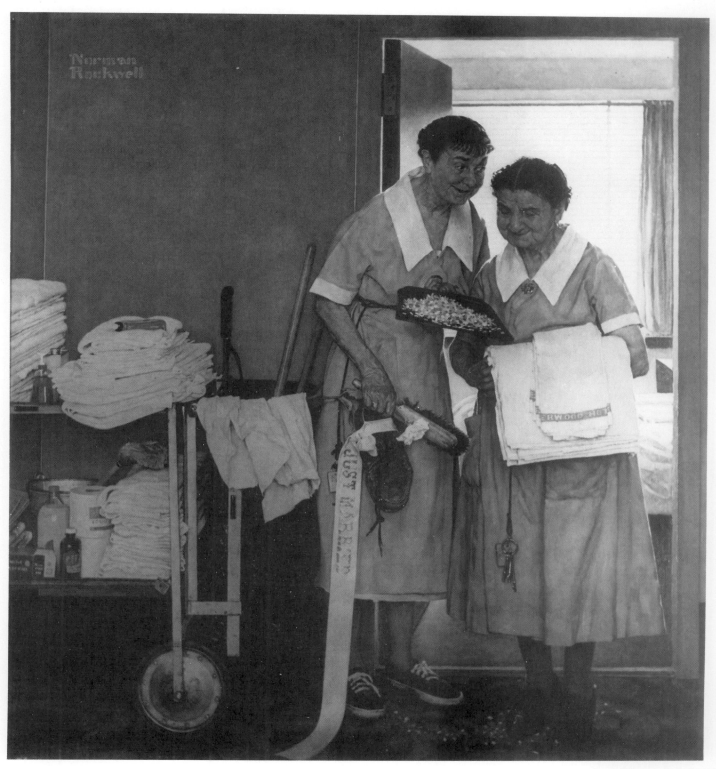

Just Married (1957)

Getting Married

Ours was not a whirlwind romance. We took our good sweet time, dating for years before we finally tied the knot. It's not that we were indecisive, though. When my sister told me that Francie was interested in me, I decided immediately to ask her out. In fact, I called her that very evening, but she'd already left for her first semester of college. I waited patiently until Thanksgiving vacation, and asked her to a movie on Friday night. An unseasonal snowstorm squelched that.

Upon her return at Christmas, we met for coffee and planned a real date for the weekend. That evening Francie got a phone call from her pregnant sister in Florida—the baby had arrived. Would Francie come down and keep her company?

During spring vacation, we finally had our first date. I remember that the movie was lousy, but as we sat in the dark I took her hand and gently squeezed it. She held onto mine for the rest of the picture. That's when I decided to marry her. We even talked about marriage that first night.

"Let's wait until neither of us is the least bit nervous about going to the courthouse. Then we'll know it's the right time and the natural thing to do." I blithely agreed. Nearly seven years later, still dating, we realized that the natural thing was to be nervous about getting married.

Now we decided that a momentous marriage proposal should be the natural culmination of a perfect and unforgettable evening. One particularly warm night, Francie and I walked out to a hillside near town. I spread out a blanket, and we lay down to gaze up at the beautiful stars. As I pointed out the Big Dipper with great authority (it's the only constellation I know), I began to suspect that this was the proposal night. Just then a heart-stopping howl from the crest of the hill had us both on our feet in time to see a mean-looking mastiff come snarling toward us. Francie, always a woman of action in the clutch, threw the blanket over the brute and we ran for our lives. Not the perfect evening.

It took us a year to give up planning The Proposal. One afternoon when Francie met me at work, we walked over to the post office to mail her latest sweepstakes entry (Francie firmly believes that she can tip the laws of probability through sheer multitude of entries). As we neared the courthouse I squeezed her hand. Without exchanging a word or a glance, we mounted the marble steps and entered the door marked "Marriage Licenses."

Making Memories

Fear kept me from retiring much earlier than I did. I wasn't sure what I would do. After fifty years of living my life around the work week, I was afraid of all the time I would have. My husband Roy, on the other hand, was downright gleeful when he announced to our family that he'd given notice.

"Two more weeks, and my time is my own! First, I'm going to put a rail fence all around the yard and plant some roses to climb up it. Then, I'm going to write a book. Maybe I'll take some cooking courses and learn how to make exotic dishes wrapped in grape leaves." He had so many plans and none of them included me.

Six months later Roy was happy as a clam. The rail fence had been built, and he was busy writing every morning. I began to resent the long commute to work. As I sat in meetings, I imagined him back home doing elaborate grocery-shopping, making a special trip to the Greek market for the grape leaves, and refinishing all the furniture in the house. I was jealous!

Then Roy discovered senior tours. We took weekend trips together to historic places, visited interesting little hotels, and went on nature walks. It hit me that after retirement, this was how I could spend all my time. Sharing day-to-day life with my husband, enjoying each other full-time. What was I waiting for?

It's been three months since my retirement, and Roy and I have made it through Italian 101 together, wallpapered three rooms, worked in a soup kitchen, shopped for a sheep farm . . . and lingered over breakfast as long as we like!

When Winter Comes (1924) 73

Shuffleton's Barbershop (1950)

Music
In America

Folk Music

Just as music incorporates single notes into a harmonious whole, so shared music binds people together as members of a group. We embrace and share songs that evoke memories of both good times and bad. Just hearing an old tune can conjure up images of youth, common causes, past passions. It is the recollection that makes the music our own and reminds us that we still belong to a group with a heritage.

Certainly America is a nation of immigrants, with each group maintaining its own culture and traditions. Yet our favorite musical pastime for the past century has been sharing our traditions. This has created a whole new body of folk music that we can truly call "uniquely American."

Folk music, the kind that is passed down from generation to generation, is an expression of the character of a people. Americans not only keep alive the memories of their homelands and traditions through a musical legacy, but they also contribute a vision of their own times, and so shape the way future Americans perceive themselves.

Gay Nineties

There is an attraction, perhaps a nostalgia, that keeps alive the sweet harmonies and quaint lyrics of the popular tunes from the turn of the century. Barbershop quartets continue to sing "Bicycle Built for Two," "Sweet Rosie O'Grady," and "Sidewalks of New York." Many of the writers of those popular songs did indeed live in New York, the gateway to America. Every morning men, women and children from Ireland, Italy, and eastern Europe poured out onto the streets of New York to seek a new beginning. They were poor in material wealth but rich in the heritage of their own languages and songs of their homelands.

Barbershop Quartet (1936)

The Music Lesson (1921)

Tin Pan Alley

There was a particular street in New York where so many of the songs America loved were written: this was 28th Street, or "Tin Pan Alley"—so nicknamed for the plinkety-plink sounds of the upright pianos that were played in virtually every music-publishing house on the street. In the first decade of the century, music publishers prospered as the sales of sheet music and piano rolls for player pianos soared. For the first time, there was truly a national audience for popular music. Although this music originated from a city of predominantly foreign-born Americans, and from a mix of ethnic sources, the country as a whole claimed it as its own.

Songwriters from Tin Pan Alley produced some of the most memorable tunes in American history, and established a popular-song genre that has continued through the present. One songwriter began as a singing waiter and "song plugger" on Tin Pan Alley, selling sheet music to music-store owners and persuading them to display it prominently. Then, the great musical sensation from the West—"Ragtime"—hit New York. Now, that plinkety-plink became a part of a ragged, syncopated new idiom.

Soldiers Singing (1918)

Wartime

A well-known American composer often wove the melodies of hymns and American folk tunes into his symphonic works. At the moment that the news of the sinking of the Lusitania reached New York, he was in the subway, and a group of New Yorkers spontaneously began singing "In the Sweet Bye and Bye." He was so moved by this common expression of grief and faith that he incorporated the melody into his next work.

During wartime, people fight, pray, and sing. During WWI, popular songs helped to boost up the spirits of Americans everywhere. Humorous songs about army life made the misery of muddy trenches almost bearable. Songwriters during both WWI and WWII produced stirring patriotic songs, marches and even upbeat dance tunes, but they did not ignore the heartbreaking realities of separation and death.

Jazz

Something happened to American music after WWI, and its name was Jazz. Jazz wasn't really the musical rebellion that so many people thought it was. The syncopation of jazz-rhythms and the improvisatory nature of jazz were elements of folk music borrowed from Afro-Americans and even eastern European immigrants. Jazz was urban folk music, an amalgamation of ragtime, blues, and myriad other musical influences.

The saxophone had been a familiar instrument to the United States since the days of military bands during the Civil War, but in the Twenties, the reedy, brassy sound of the saxophone became a smooth and soaring singing voice in the jazz band.

The violinist in Rockwell's painting gazes at the instrument with curiosity and a bit of wonder. His threadbare clothes bespeak of his commitment, despite hardship, to his art. November 1929 was a difficult time to find a job, especially as a classical musician. "What if I were starting all over today?" he seems to wonder. "Would I be playing jazz on a saxophone?"

Man Looking at Saxophone (1929)

It Don't Mean a Thing If It Ain't Got That Swing

Swing was both melodic and brash at the same time, spontaneous and impulsive, with a driving beat that made it supremely danceable. The big-band sound was just what the doctor ordered. America had contracted dance fever, and it could only be relieved by a frenetic dance—the jitterbug. In every dance palace and ballroom across the country, couples cut loose to the sounds of big bands. Swing singers enthralled audiences everywhere, and reached even wider audiences over radio.

The ailing record industry was able to pull itself up by the bootstraps thanks to a machine that offered the big band tunes for a nickel per shot— the automatic phonograph commonly called the jukebox. With the repeal of Prohibition in 1934, newly-reopened bars, restaurants and cafes installed the machines and found that customers were more than willing to pay to hear popular songs. Dancing to the music tended to make patrons thirsty, and this further increased business.

Jukeboxes of the time were designed to be the focal point of a room, just as if a live band were playing onstage. They reflected the glamourous style of the big band stars, and bespangled dance palaces with glowing colored lights, bubbling liquids, and gold and glitter cabinets.

Swing became such a phenomenon that it inspired a language called "Jive." Hepcats and alligators (swing enthusiasts) cut a rug (danced) while skin beaters (drummers), canaries (vocalists) and the cat with the licorice stick (clarinetist) or the plumbing (trumpet or trombone player) put everyone in the groove.

Of course, love songs will always be with us, and many tunes from the Thirties are still well-known and touching today.

The ukelele, commonplace in the Twenties, made a comeback in the Thirties . . . partly because it was portable and easy to play, but also because a very popular radio personality played one. Sheet music for the pop hits often included chord charts for the ukelele so that crooners could strum along.

Country Western Music

One day in 1927, a fellow stepped up to the microphone in a radio station in Asheville, North Carolina, strummed his guitar and sang what was called "hillbilly music." Until then, few record companies had considered country music to be marketable. But within a year that "hillbilly music" was selling like hotcakes.

Some songs were called "blue yodels"—a mix of blues, Appalachian folk or hillbilly music, and usually a chorus of yodeling. Another young singer imitated this style and yodel. His popularity and the popularity of country music spread until Hollywood saw a good thing and offered this cowboy singer a contract.

Such cowboy songs were not authentic country-western tunes, but were written by the same Tin Pan Alley songwriters who wrote all the other popular music. These orchestrated hits were only a faint echo of the grit and integrity of real cowboy songs, originally sung in a plaintive, nasally voice about hardship and heartbreak. Nevertheless, the songs written by industry songwriters became cowboy favorites.

It certainly wasn't hard to understand why rural America found country-western music appealing. But perhaps urban America enjoyed it because the independence and freedom of life on the range afforded a nostalgic look at a young country before big city problems; when nature, rather than the stock market, determined the conditions of survival. Some songs poked fun at all the city greenhorns and their romanticizing of the Old West. But even suave, urban-intellectual songwriters couldn't resist writing "cowboy" tunes. Cowboy music, both authentic and urban, remains an important part of our heritage.

Cowboy with Gramophone (1927)

Happy Songs

The Great Depression was one of the darkest times in American history—terrifying for the many homeless who existed from day to day by virtue of the soup kitchen. But, perhaps not surprisingly, this era produced some of America's most optimistic and cheerful songs. In times of despair, these were the songs people wanted to hear.

It wasn't denial or escapism that turned the public's ears toward the bright side, but rather the desperately firm belief that prosperity **was** right around the corner. The Old World may have looked constantly to its past, but Americans were in the habit of anticipating their future.

Toward the end of the Thirties, young people were bored with what they called "schmaltz and corn" music, and began to yearn for a more energetic musical direction. They found it in a sound that came rumbling, then roaring out of the jazz of the Twenties. It was called "swing."

Music Education—The Recital

When I first laid eyes on the sheet music for my recital piece, "Indian Drums," I had a sinking feeling that this was a crossroads for the piano and me. My music teacher, Mrs. Hall, had been patient for a whole year but it was becoming apparent that she did not expect me to become a concert pianist. Let's face it; I can't rub my head and pat my stomach at the same time—and for a pianist, that spells washout.

Hitchhiker (1940)

The Costume

As I practiced "Indian Drums" week after week, I became mesmerized by that throbbing left-hand rhythm. Meanwhile, my mother prepared for the recital, too. She let down the hem on my pink party dress and added an overskirt of dotted swiss to make it "more dramatic." A broad pink sash was a necessity; so was a pink satin hair bow that made me look as if I were wearing a dinner plate on the side of my head. Last but not least was a pair of brand-new patent-leather shoes with bows. I think it was Mother's way of blocking out the incessant BOM . . . bom, bom, bom of "Indian Drums." Surely if I had the correct costume and put my best foot forward, musical talent would naturally follow.

On day of the recital, my mother told me that even famous performers had butterflies before a performance. She vigorously ironed my over-starched dress so that when I put it on, it crunched in a pleasant way when I walked. My patent leathers were so shiny that when they caught the light they were dazzling. I wasn't really nervous, I was merely numb. This was the day of reckoning, the day I would be publicly humiliated for not practicing enough. I suppose that's why my mother dressed me like an angel with a sash tied in a bow so big that you'd think I had pink wings. We both hoped that the audience might go easy on me.

The Performance

As the other budding concert pianists played their pieces, I watched Mrs. Hall's face. She was all smiles, nodding and applauding as each student took a bow. Now it was my turn. I tried to think about how Shirley Temple would have eagerly tap-danced up the steps to the stage, but all I could hear was the deafening crunch! crunch! of my starched skirt as I slowly crossed to the piano and carefully slid onto the piano bench. I let my wrists go limp and raised my hands, dropping them on the keys. (Mrs. Hall said I had such a pretty way of doing that—just like a bird alighting.) At that point I began to panic. I looked up and saw Mrs. Hall, her body rigid, a smile frozen on her face. The keys were swimming before my eyes. This was the punishment for pretending to have musical ability!

Then that throbbing left hand rhythm came over me. Again and again I thumped the keys . . . BOM . . . bom, bom, bom. The mystical power of the tom-tom took hold. After two minutes of that, my vision cleared and I became aware of a certain restlessness in the audience. But my disembodied hands just kept playing. "How can I make this end? Will I be trapped in 'Indian Drums' forever?" The thought made me stand up with a start, and a grateful audience showered me with applause. As I took my bow, I caught sight of my reflection in those brand-new patent-leather shoes with the bows. There was a look a triumph on my face. After this hair-raising experience, my mother would never again insist that I learn to play a musical instrument!

Piano Tuner (1947)

Trumpet Lessons

I was ten years old when the school sent home a form asking my parents which instrument their son would like to learn to play in the school orchestra. So far as I was concerned, there were only three choices—drums, trombone or trumpet. My father winced when he heard my choices, and immediately vetoed the drums. My mother even suggested I take up the flute, of all things. I realized that my parents were not facing reality!

Actually, there had been a time when I was not aware of these realities myself. At five years old, before I knew any better, I had fallen in love with the violin. I'd seen a gypsy violinist on television and was struck by the hauntingly beautiful sound of the instrument. I wanted a violin in the worst way, so I finally made one for myself from a cereal box and rubber bands.

As it happened, the trumpet was actually an excellent choice. During those formative years, it helped me develop fat lips and a great set of lungs, for there is no such thing as a small effort in trumpet-playing. In order to get a sound out of it, one must blow with all one's might, turning purple in the face and weak in the knees. Physically, it was exhausting to practice. That is why my mother would allow only ten minutes of practice per day (at least that was the reason she gave).

For some students, practicing was not a physical challenge; carrying the instrument home was the hard part. Milt Benson, the smallest kid in the class, picked the cello as his instrument. He won new respect from the guys for being able to lug that thing back and forth for a whole school year. He also gained incredible biceps for a ten-year-old!

At our first orchestra concert, three selections were listed on the program—but only two of them were recognizable when we played them. The first was "Twinkle Twinkle Little Star" and the other was "Ain't We Got Fun." "The Saints Go Marching In" featured so much booming bass drum, wheezy squeaking of clarinets and sawing of violins, that we sounded like a junkyard strapped to a lumbering elephant with asthma! But it didn't really matter whether anyone could follow the tune. Just to be a part of all that sound was so satisfying that the following year I signed up for tuba!

Boy Practicing Trumpet (1950)

Aunt Ella Takes a Trip (1942)

America
in Motion

Before the Automobile

Before the turn of the century, travel involved a long and arduous journey by horse, buggy, stagecoach, train or boat. Dirt roads were rough and rides were bumpy. When it rained, buggy wheels sank in the mud; certainly people did not travel for the pleasure of it! Life throughout most of the country was relatively sedentary. One belonged to a group that was bound by the distance one could travel in a day—these were neighbors. A family drove to church, to town, or perhaps to visit relatives, but mostly folks stayed at home. Tourism was enjoyed mainly by the rich, who could afford luxury accommodations on trains and ships.

The end of the next decade saw the mass-production of an invention that would change everything—the automobile. The car allowed the average American to achieve a mobility that he never dreamed was possible. It drastically broadened our world view and changed forever our concept of the term "neighbor." For better or for worse, the lives of all Americans are now intimately bound with the automobile.

Early Motoring

The first "horseless carriage" was a three-wheeled, open buggy with a gas-powered engine under the seat. Instead of reins, one used a tiller or lever to steer the car. The headlamps were candled-powered, just as they had been on stagecoaches and carriages for years. Indeed, cars were handmade with all the detailing and accoutrements of fine coaches, and purchased by those wealthy enough to afford the expensive but notoriously unreliable playthings. One car boasted an "8 H.P. double-opposed motor and double tube tires" while another featured "sensitive steering wheel, graceful design, handsome in finish and appointments." The price was $850.

But for all the assuring advertising copy, "Be prepared" was the motorist's motto. The toolbox was an essential part of the car because breakdowns were frequent; flat tires were commonplace. Of course, with no gas stations, a motorist had to carry his own fuel. Roads at the time were bumpy and dusty, or muddy. The required costume for men was a dust coat, peaked hat, goggles, scarf and heavy gloves. Women also wore dusters, long veils to cover face and neck, and gauntlets.

Those who took up the hobby of motoring often had to deal with the hostility of the general public. Cars were noisy. They spooked horses, killed chickens and even knocked down pedestrians.

By 1905, despite all the inconveniences, ten thousand car-owners in the United States enjoyed the sport of motoring. A ride in a motor car was truly an adventure, and all the more thrilling when one could race down the road at fifteen or even twenty miles per hour!

Then in 1908 an important event ushered us into the automotive age: After the manner in which livestock were handled in the slaughterhouses of Chicago, the idea of automotive mass-production was formulated right after the first Model T was manufactured. An assembly-line system of manufacturing eventually revolutionized industry world-wide. Products could be made more cheaply and thus be priced within the reach of the common man. Now, motoring was no longer the exclusive hobby of the rich. Seventeen hundred "Tin Lizzies," as they were fondly called, were sold in the first year of production. By the time the last Model T rolled off the assembly line twenty years later, the American people had bought fifteen million of them.

Couple in Early Auto (1924)

Meanwhile, other car companies were following Ford's lead in mass-production and making refinements in design as well. A development that helped to sell the idea of motoring to women was the electric self-starter. This meant no more sore arms from car cranks. In the advertisements, cleanliness and ease of operation were the selling features that appealed to women. The disadvantage was that the battery-powered vehicle was useful only on well-paved roads and short trips. It was a "shopping" car.

Another new and improved car had a "self-ventilating, rain-vision windshield," and mohair, leather-edged convertible top. One top-of-the-line manufacturer introduced the idea of interchangeable parts. The company described its car as "the difference between traveling and traveling in luxury." Car manufacturers won over the American people with promises of performance, comfort, and finally, affordability. By 1920, one in every thirteen American families owned a car.

The Family Car

On Sunday afternoon, the idea of a jaunt in the car was irresistible. The trouble was, would-be Sunday drivers often had no place to go. It wasn't that Americans couldn't think of a destination, but that roads suitable for motoring were still few and far between.

Most roads were so bad that it was necessary to load down the back of the car for traction, cross your fingers and hope that the next state had at least a layer of gravel. Many of the state highway departments could not pave fast enough. The Federal Highway Act of 1921 began a national highway system that was paving ten thousand miles of road a year by 1930. Now, a cross-country traveler could drive all the way from New York to Kansas on a paved road before it turned to dirt again.

The Twenties also saw the flowering of roadside advertising. Still-famous billboards sprouted up along the new U.S. routes and delighted weary travellers with their homespun humor and their clever ditties designed to entertain.

The birth of the motel industry was foretold in a series of magazine articles describing a chain of small, clean, pleasant hotels, standardized and nationally advertised, along every important motor route in the country. Roadside stands popped up, renting out campsites and overnight tourist cabins to motorists. A family with a home along a highway could put out a "tourist home" sign and take in overnight guests for a charge. Depending upon one's scruples, these could be either a real bargain or a motorist's nightmare.

Trio in Early Motor Car (1920)

Scandalous to many were the effects the automobile had upon young people. As the early open motor cars gave way to closed sedans, the car became the means of escape from the watchful eyes of small-town observers and constant supervision. A closed car was a traveling room that could take a young person down the highway to the next town, or to a roadhouse where he was suddenly a stranger. With this anonymity came the opportunity to whoop it up without anyone back home finding out about it. Although the automobile was not the only reason for what was considered a decline in morals and manners in the younger generation of the Jazz Age, it certainly contributed.

During the early Twenties—and indeed ever since—the car has been a status symbol. While luxurious homes were once the sign of having "arrived," the luxury automobile was now a superior mobile status symbol. It gave the car-owner a feeling of power and mastery that made reverting to streetcar-travel unthinkable.

The Rumbleseat

Gazing at the landscape through the small peephole windows of a carriage might have been stimulating for the ladies of the previous century, but modern girls preferred to climb into the rumbleseats for a more exciting ride. The sports roadster with a rumbleseat was the choice car of both the young and the young-at-heart. Not only was it cheaper than touring cars, but it had other attractions as well. One had to be young and agile to step high enough to reach the top of the back fender, swing over and drop into the seat. Despite the awkward entry, the rumbleseat maintained its popular reputation throughout the Thirties as the thrilling—if uncomfortable—place to ride.

The development of new kinds of steel, as well as synthetic materials, changed the design and the shape of the automobile in the Thirties. Now, it was possible to smooth out the angles and streamline the car body. The boxy look of the earlier cars was out. The car was its own machine; no longer was it necessary to mimic the horseless carriage of the past. The inventions of new suspensions, bumpers, safety glass, turn signals and electric windshield wipers, along with better engine design, all screamed "modern."

Smoother lines could also be observed in buildings, furniture, appliances

Couple in Rumbleseat (1935)

and women's fashions. The smooth, streamlined styling prevailed throughout the Thirties . . . and yet the term used to describe a superior car was still "sharp!"

Portrait of Charles A. Lindbergh

On the wet morning of May 20, 1927, a young airmail pilot from the West took off from Roosevelt Field in New York in a single-engine plane called "Spirit of St. Louis" bound for Paris, France. From the moment the plane left the ground in a sluggish takeoff that left anxious witnesses gasping, this flight captured the imaginations of the American people. Newspapers and radio were ecstatic in their reports of the lone pilot's progress. Suspense mounted until he was sighted off the Irish coast, then crossing the Channel—and finally, landing at Le Bourget airport 33 1/2 hours later where was greeted by an exuberant crowd of Parisians.

It was as if Charles A. Lindbergh had pulled a cork—the outpouring of enthusiasm for his achievement was more spectacular than anything seen before or since. Upon his return to America, the country came to a standstill for days just to applaud its new hero. There were parades down Fifth Avenue, receptions, lavish dinners, and countless telegrams of congratulations. President Coolidge presented Lindbergh with the Distinguished Flying Cross, the Congressional Medal of Honor, and a commission as a colonel in the Officer Reserve Corps, and said, "You've broken down the barriers of time and space and brought two great peoples into closer communion." Lindbergh's feat made giant headlines in every newspaper in America. Songs and poems were composed in his honor. His picture was hung on classroom walls across the country as a model for children. Here was a fine-looking young man of quiet charm, modest and courageous, who turned down offers to cash in on his fame, and never sought the limelight. He was a perfect hero and an embodiment of everything that Americans wanted to be. He stood for individualism in the face of an increasingly conformist society. He was a pioneer who restored our national pride.

Pioneer of the Air (1927)

Passenger Air Travel

Only one short decade after Lindbergh's historic flight, air travel was within reach of anyone who could afford a ticket. In 1929, coast-to-coast air service was introduced. At that time, passengers did not spend the entire duration of the trip in the air. They took a night train from New York to Chicago, were driven from the station to an airfield, and flown from there to Oklahoma. From that landing field, they were driven to yet another train station for an overnight trip to New Mexico, and then finally flown from there to Los Angeles. This 48-hour ordeal was called "New York to Los Angeles service!"

In 1936 the first DC 3s were put into service between New York and Chicago. The all-metal planes carried twenty-one passengers and had a maximum airspeed of 200 miles per hour, as well as the distinct advantage of being able to fly above the weather. They were very popular planes with the airlines; one aircraft company built ten thousand of them.

The grandmother in Rockwell's painting gazes at the passing clouds, through the window of a new DC-3, with a look of restrained excitement and anticipation. She has seen many changes in her lifetime; having been born just after the Civil War, she has lived through horse-and-buggy days, the invention of the telephone, the lightbulb, the automobile, the first airplanes, and the radio. She has watched her country endure the War-To-End-All-Wars, and the Great Depression thereafter. Human triumphs and suffering have both touched her life . . . and yet she looks eagerly toward the future.

She has just begun her cross-country flight—perhaps to visit relatives, or to take the airline at its word and "See America from the Air." The map on her lap indicates her route in red grease pencil, and reveals that she might be bound for Arizona. A long trip lies ahead, with many stops for maintenance and refueling. But the speed and comfort of air travel have made this trip possible for an old woman. It's obvious that she welcomes the adventure.

Old Woman Riding Airplane (1938)

Union Station, Chicago (1944)

Train Travel

The war put a big strain on the railroads. Every train was pressed into service as a troop train, or to carry war materiel. Passenger trains were crowded; you were lucky to find a seat—and uniforms lay everywhere. The trains were full of soldiers, sailors, and marines going home on leave or being transported from one base to another. You could always identify those who were coming from bootcamp; they were the ones with the shortest haircuts. It wasn't long before we all became familiar with rank insignia and the various stripes, and could distinguish a first lieutenant, a second lieutenant, a major and a colonel from one another.

Many people travelled during the war. Families gave up their homes and apartments in order to move closer to the men on the bases. War brides followed their husbands from camp to camp. Women got war jobs and had to leave their children with parents or in-laws. Uprooting and separation became the norm.

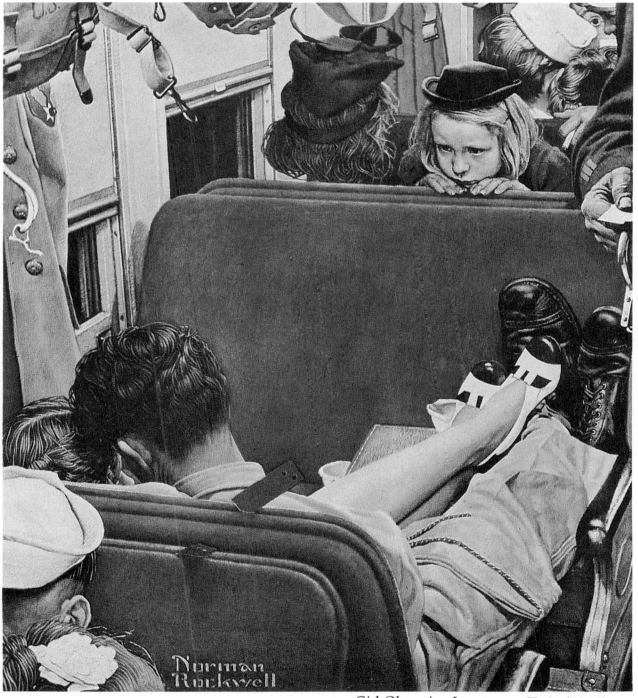

Girl Observing Lovers on a Train (1944)

The compartments of most commuter trains featured benches screwed to the floor and a single bare lightbulb for illumination. People often sat on the floor. Refreshments on these train were limited. They generally consisted of ham sandwiches, cheese sandwiches, or ham-and-cheese sandwiches on not-so-fresh white bread, and coffee. Of course, since there were very few club cars, a man in a white coat delivered refreshments in a basket.

The major train stations acted as a hub, a great exchange. Such activity might have been exciting if one were able to avert the terrible cloud of uncertainty that hung over all. Everywhere couples stood embracing after long separations, or exchanging tearful goodbyes. Such scenes were often heartbreaking.

Post-war Buying

Many Americans were afraid that even though the United States had escaped the devastation suffered by European nations, adjusting to a peacetime economy would spell hardship for the American people. Where would all the returning GIs find jobs? How could factories make a quick switch from producing tanks and munitions to providing consumer goods once again? During the years immediately after the war, inflation and unemployment caused widespread fear of another depression, perhaps as awful as the one before. But, to the country's relief, the economy found a balance and Americans began to prosper as never before.

The GI Bill of Rights was instrumental in easing the returning soldier's adjustment to peacetime. Through the GI Bill, he received job counseling and placement, tuition and living expenses while in school, and loans to start new business. Stability returned to the American family—and with it, a desire for the Good Life that the war had postponed.

As with all wars, WWII lasted longer than anyone had anticipated. For years, rationing of gasoline and tires and the unavailability of new cars had forced Americans to wait, save and continually patch up their old rattletraps to keep them on the road. But sacrifice and saving had made Americans hungry for new homes, new clothes, and new cars. Postwar housing demands were staggering. Suburbs sprouted up outside every city and became occupied as fast as developers could build them. The garment industry could barely keep up with the new demand for casual clothes. Household appliances such as clothes dryers, garbage disposals and dishwashers appeared in more and more American homes. Car manufacturers were not far behind. 1947 saw the first new car to be produced after the war. It wasn't particularly remarkable in design, but anxious customers snatched up every car that rolled off the assembly line. The other

Fixing a Flat (1946)

auto manufacturers soon followed suit and introduced their own new models—big cars with V-8 engines that sold for an average of $1,800. By 1949, car dealers had sold over five million cars, and once again the proud car owner rolled down the road on four brand-new tires in his shiny new status symbol.

Portrait of An Astronaut

I didn't understand it at first. I didn't speak Norwegian, so for the life of me I couldn't understand why so many other hotel guests all grinned at me, slapped me on the back, shook my hand. "What friendly people," I thought. Then the desk clerk came running across the lobby of the hotel with a copy of an English newspaper. On the front page, the headlines shrieked, "American Astronauts Walk on the Moon!" I gasped, then grinned back at the dozen beaming faces. We just couldn't stop smiling at one another.

At breakfast, there was a tiny American flag on each table. The chef peered out from the kitchen as I selected my breakfast fish, and could contain himself no longer—he rushed out with a cry of glee to shake my hand. We were all part of this celebration. All day, recognized as an American, I was congratulated with hugs, cheers, and handshakes. Waves of sheer pride swept over me and sent chills down my back. Americans had done something that awed mankind. The pioneer spirit was alive.

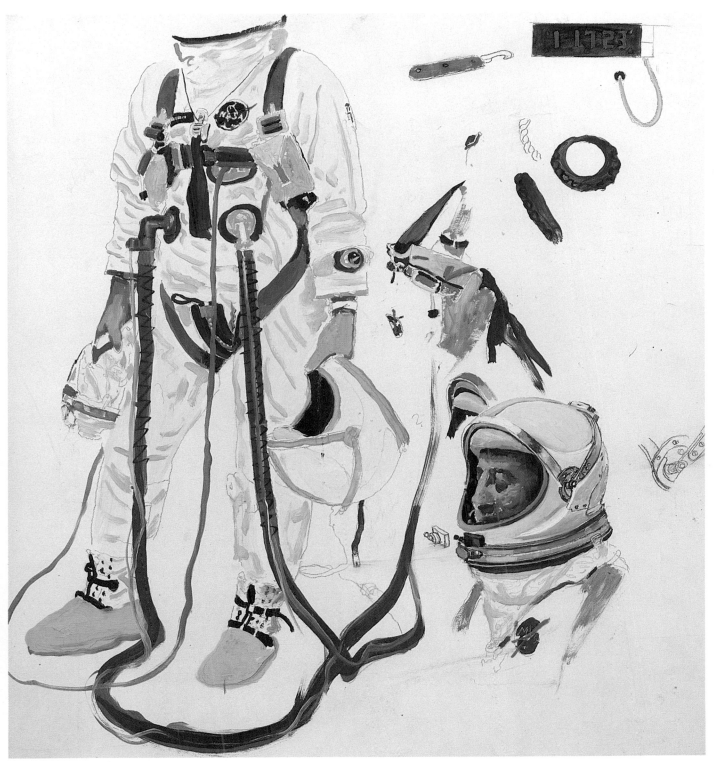

The Longest Step (1965)

America at the Polls (1944)

Politics
in America

The Debate

I was nine years old, a fourth grader at Prescott Elementary that election year when the PTA gave students a chance to see how the American electoral process worked. A mock presidential debate was scheduled to take place at the monthly PTA meeting. I was chosen to be the stand-in for Adlai Stevenson, and Janet Spargo was Dwight D. Eisenhower.

The debate got off to an oppressive start: Janet was a good foot taller than I was, and there were some giggles from the audience as we took the stage. I was decked out in my orange-and-green-striped corduroy jacket and bow tie, and I had done my homework. I remember making the point that because Adlai Stevenson's grandfather was Grover Cleveland's vice president, Stevenson had White House experience. That revelation produced a light smattering of applause.

Then I caught sight of my father, in the third row, absolutely glowing with pride! I guess that's when the crusader spirit hit me. All the passionate energy of the underdog came welling up. This David was going to beat Goliath! My voice nearly cracked several times as I delivered what I thought was an amazingly eloquent speech about American ideals and human rights. I felt I grew a foot taller as I embodied the dignity and integrity of the man I was representing. Our cause would prevail! As Janet responded, I felt she lacked the necessary zeal. Surely the victory would go to Stevenson.

But the audience thought otherwise . . . and so did the voting public. Adlai Stevenson lost the election. I felt so bad about it that I wrote Mr. Stevenson a letter telling him how sorry I was about the loss, but that I hoped he wouldn't give up and would run again. He—or probably his secretary—wrote me a letter assuring me that he would try again for the presidency.

Barbecues and Clambakes

I'm not sure how it happened, but my brother became a driver for a major local political figure. Bud first encountered the fellow at a meeting of the Shamrock Democratic Club in the basement of a tavern. Mack claimed that he had no driver's license, but that he was working on the City Comptroller's campaign and needed to get around town.

"A bright kid like you . . ." he said to Bud, "hey, stick with me. You want to be a Liquor Board inspector? Well, maybe when you turn twenty-one. Maybe 'til then we could get you in the House of Delegates. What do you say?"

After that, Bud went to a lot of barbecues and clambakes all over the city with Mack. He drove and Mack rode in the back of Dad's '55 Chevy and smoked smelly cigars. My father complained about the stench but Bud told him he was getting an invaluable political education. It was true.

One night, Mack had my brother drive him to a political rally at a club in one of the shabbiest areas of the city. This place had a reputation for being dangerous in broad daylight, let alone after dark! There was no place to park except an open spot in front of a fire hydrant. "Pull in here," said Mack.

"But what if I get a ticket?" Bud asked.

"I'll take care of it. Just pull in," he insisted. They were late already. My brother told me that when he walked into the club there was a mayoral candidate standing on the bar making a speech to a group of "ladies of the evening" about garbage collection in the city. They seemed to be interested. Other politicos arrived and spoke well into the night.

Elect Casey (1958)

When they finally emerged from the club, a police officer was standing next to my father's car, writing a ticket.

"Hi, Mack, good to see you," said the officer. Mack waited patiently while the officer wrote out the ticket. Bud's heart sank. He said it wasn't paying the ticket that he minded, but the fact that my father would get a copy in the mail with the time of day and the questionable address. He'd have a lot of explaining to do.

Then Mack grabbed the ticket and said, "I'll take care of this."

He did, too. He had the fine reduced to $1 and paid it. Then, as he handed the receipt to Bud, he said, "Now how about doing me a favor?" It seemed that there was some door-to-door campaigning to do in a neighborhood where Mack thought that clean-cut young people, like the ones Bud knew, would present the best image.

My brother enlisted his girlfriend and a half-dozen other people from school. He let me tag along, too. I remember the speech he delivered to the others about how important it is to get involved and be a part of the political process. Then Mack arrived with a man that never smiled or said a word. He just pulled a huge roll of bills out of his pocket, peeled off $200, and handed it to Bud. I thought it was an unsettling moment as Bud stood, clutching a wad of money in his hand, between those old-fashioned political bosses and the fresh faces of these new activists.

All day we walked up and down streets, ringing doorbells and talking to voters. It was a political education in itself. That evening Bud gave $5 to each worker, including me, and then Bud and I drove over to see Mack and give him back the rest of the money. He was surprised to see us. "You keep that money," he said.

"Why not just put it back where it came from?" Bud asked.

"I **can't** put it back!" he said emphatically. "You share it with the boys."

When the election returns started coming in, it was apparent that we had a new City Comptroller. Our candidate had lost his job. I'm sure Mack scrambled to make the most of the situation . . . but all I know is that he had to find a new driver.

The American Dream

I had just turned fourteen when Mother and Dad decided to spring the news on us at dinner: we were moving—and in less than two months. My sister Katie was only eight then, so the prospect wasn't quite so frightening to her. I'd been looking forward to freshman year at Jefferson High since Christmas though, and now it seemed as if my world had just been turned upside-down. I'd finally made some really special friends—and Lisa, the girl I'd been staring at for eight months, had finally begun to stare back . . .

I should have known it was coming. For almost a year, Mother and Dad had talked about nothing else. I knew that Dad was expecting a big raise—but when it finally came through, it didn't occur to me right away that this meant everything would change.

Moving In (1967)

On the day Dad drove us across town to show us the new house, I finally realized why that raise had been so important: this house was going to represent everything my parents had ever hoped for together, and at last their biggest dream had come true! Who was I to mope around while this was happening?

113

The house was beautiful—and big! While Katie was busy explaining to Dad exactly what color she wanted her room painted, I remember strolling out to the back yard, trying to experience the feeling that I was really "at home." It wasn't easy, yet—the place was empty and smelled like paint, and the newly-planted little trees out back were no more than sticks. But, if I really tried, I could picture myself barbecuing here with Dad and a new friend or two. And Katie's Brownie Scout troop could have a ball out here, "camping out" in the spacious safety of our new suburban back yard! This might just begin to feel like home after all . . .

The weeks flew by as the big day approached. There was so much to be done! I never realized how many things we'd accumulated during all those years in our small apartment—until I saw how many boxes we needed to hold everything. The night before, I walked through each room, hardly recognizing this place where I'd spent so many years. It was my way of saying goodbye.

Moving day arrived—and, strange as it seems, the whole day was just one big blur for me. But that night, as I sat alone in my new room after the day's activity, I realized—just as my parents had realized the day my father accepted that raise—that nothing lay before me except opportunity. I wasn't leaving behind my old life; I was sitting right here with it scattered around me. Instead, I was beginning a new one.

The Issues

Word got out at the pancake breakfast. The land at the top of the ridge had been sold to a developer, and would be divided into lots for luxury homes. No one expressed disbelief; the history of political corruption in the county had long since destroyed any illusions.

For a moment the breakfasters in the room were merely grim. Our fund-raiser had garnered $600. The developer had bought the ridge for two million. We had no power to protect woods, streams or trails that we had walked seeking a quiet refuge from highways and malls. Luxury homes. What a shame.

Our Nature Center Council called for a public meeting. There were still some of us who believed that public outcry and especially television cameras might have an effect on the developer's plans. A stockbroker suggested that we lie down in front of the bulldozers. An older woman in an

Freedom of Speech (1943) 115

Icelandic sweater wanted to start a petition right away. Some old hands in development battles wanted strategy sessions and meetings with County Water and Sewer people. "We need a lawyer! A lawyer!" called out an old man in the back.

The president of the Council recognized someone from the floor, a small fellow with an even smaller, world-weary overcoat pulled up around his neck and buttoned up to the chin. His eyes behind his thick glasses were watery and red-rimmed as he rose and spoke:

"Shame on us if we don't do everything we can to save this natural treasure for our children," he said in his quiet, raspy voice. "Our park seems big today, but one day very soon it will be a tiny island surrounded by a sea of development. How could we face our children and grandchildren if we allowed the profit motive to destroy their land? How can the County do this? Shame on them. Shame on us if we don't do everything in our power to save this small piece of paradise, **our** piece, from greedy hands."

It was only a short speech, but it left most of us with lumps in our throats. How had a group of jaded suburbanites become so attached to the land? Was it because of our vague recollections of childhood moments spent rolling in piles of crunchy autumn leaves, or wading in ankle-numbing streams on a hot summer day? Those streams **were** getting increasingly more difficult to find. Our children may find them only in dreams.

Difference of Opinion

Mom and Dad almost never argued—not that they didn't have disagreements. Sometimes Mom would get angry and yell about how she couldn't handle the house and the cooking, her full-time job **and** the Christmas shopping too! But Dad never yelled back. We'd all take cover until her temper cooled, then we'd contritely pick up our dirty clothes while Dad went in to do the dishes. I wouldn't call that an argument.

But every four years a cloud would drift across the sky at our house. As the primaries approached, Mom joked about how she would pick a winner to beat the candidate chosen by Dad's party. At first it would amount to just a gentle ribbing, but after the primaries and conventions were over, the battle lines were drawn.

Breakfast Table Political Argument (1948)

At breakfast Mom would start reading Dad's candidate's quotations from the paper in a voice dripping with sarcasm. Dad would retaliate by insinuating that no bleeding-heart liberal, especially a woman, could understand the simple truths about economics. Mom's voice would rise in pitch as she ticked off facts and figures (Mom has an excellent memory for any statistics she reads) while Dad would nod impatiently waiting for my mother to finish saying all the while, "Be that as it may . . ."

While the coffee and toast grew cold, the debate grew hot. When my father began to stutter with repressed emotion we knew it was time to divert one of them. My know-it-all sister would say, "I don't know why you're even arguing about it; your votes will just cancel each other's out." My parents would respond by staring daggers at my sister.

The other mine field was the living room, where Mom and Dad watched the six o'clock news. "Look at him, just look at him, Marjorie," Dad would say. "He's a wimp and he doesn't know a thing about foreign affairs.

"Nonsense, Phil, he knows that 62.3 billion dollars in military spending isn't going to help us compete with the Japanese," my mother would respond. Soon no one was watching the news because you couldn't hear it above the shouting. By contrast, dinner would be eaten in total silence while my parents' anger seethed.

What was really remarkable was that on election night, as my parents sat watching the election results on television, we never heard, "I told you so," or self-congratulations of any sort. There was no haggling about the campaign or the issues. The storm was over. Now, all that mattered was to comfort the despondent loser. They'd sit like lovebirds on the sofa, arms around each other, and plan a weekend trip or a night on the town together.

The next morning at breakfast, the newspaper was nowhere to be seen. As my mother nibbled her toast, Dad complained about the squirrels on the bird feeder. "They scare away all the chickadees," he moaned. We welcomed the squirrels like a breath of fresh air—all those political shadows were finally gone!

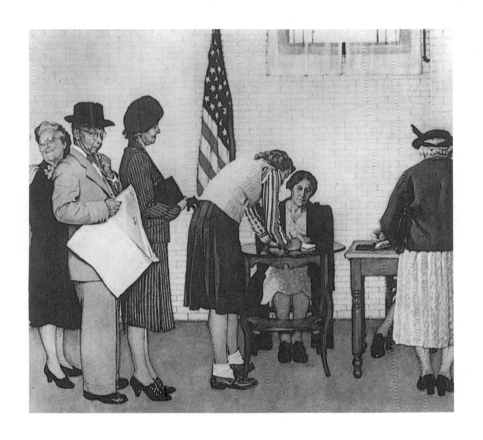

Election Day (1944)

Election Day

I'm not sure why, but when I vote on election day, I feel as if the world is whispering, "Bob Thornton, we know you exist." It's like being in the telephone book. When the woman behind the table opens that big book and runs her finger down the page, she finds my name. "Yes, Mr. Thornton—will you please sign here?"

But voting goes beyond that, since the telephone company doesn't ask me for my opinion. Maybe it's limited to "yes" and "no," but when I vote I am registering my opinion. When I watch the returns on election night, I see 3,456,012 votes, not 3,456,011. The difference, however small, was because of me. My voice counts.

My one vote is just as important as the one vote from the candidate himself. As I stand in my paint-covered work clothes by the curtained booth, the lawyer and the businesswoman in suits, the elderly jogger in her lavender sweatsuit join me in line—and regardless of income or influence, we all have an equal voice in the booth. To pull down that lever is to put your choice on the record—it's making history.

Some people say it's a waste of time to vote, that one vote makes no difference, or that the system is corrupt and the most powerful political machines always win. I think such people are afraid to claim any responsibility for what happens. They are afraid to delegate power to a representative or to vote on an issue and risk being wrong. You must exercise the right to vote if you want to keep your political muscle in shape.

My fellow voters are always congenial and especially polite at the polls. Maybe it's the curtain and the privacy of the decision that contributes to the extra courtesy. Everyone is patient, and the line is orderly—not like the line at the supermarket! Perhaps it's because we all understand that voting is a duty.

My mother told me that for years the only reason she voted was that women had won the vote the hard way. Voting was a symbol to her, a tribute to those who suffered so long without a voice. "How could I **not** vote when I think of all those silent ones?" she mused.

Voting Booth (1944)

The Inauguration

The crackling voice of the weather man on the bus radio reported that there were eighteen inches of snow on the ground in Washington. Someone whistled softly. We pretended to be blase, worldly college men, but we were all secretly thrilled to be marching in the inaugural parade—especially Kennedy's inaugural parade. Ironically, on that bitter cold day in January, my ROTC unit was representing the bright and balmy Virgin Islands, which couldn't afford to send their own representatives.

Our battered school bus pulled into a parking lot near the Washington Monument, where the other buses were also unloading marchers. We wore our dress uniforms, with rifles and shoes polished and gleaming as we stepped out into the brittle air. We discovered that ours was the last group in that long parade down windswept Pennsylvania Avenue. We spent most of the day trying to keep warm, stamping our feet to see if we could restore the feeling back to them. Once we were actually marching, though, it was a lot easier.

As we approached the presidential reviewing stand, I stole my first glance at the President of the United States. Even from that distance, I could clearly see his face! We paused to perform our extravaganza rifle-twirling demonstration that we'd practiced all year, and received some enthusiastic applause even from that frostbitten crowd. Then, as we marched past him, I saw President Kennedy lift his silk top hat in salute.

We were a boisterous gang of nineteen-year-old kids as we returned home. With the bus heater cranked up high, and our spirits even higher, we celebrated our third-place award, the inauguration of **our** President, and the feeling that this was exactly the right time to be entering adulthood. With our help, the country—the **world**—had a chance to make a fresh start. Together, we were going to do great things.

Norman Rockwell

JFK's Bold Legacy (1966) 123

Picture Credits:

Triple Self Portrait, 1960, endsheets, courtesy of Norman Rockwell Paintings Trust at Old Corner House, Stockbridge, Massachusetts.

Boy on High Dive, 1947, page 16, courtesy of Martin Diamond Fine Arts, New York, New York.

Shaftsbury Blacksmith Shop, 1940, page 32, courtesy of the Berkshire Museum, Pittsfield, Massachusetts.

Full Treatment, 1940, page 35, courtesy of Judy Goffman Fine Art, New York, New York.

Crestwood Commuter Station, 1946, page 40, courtesy of Christie's, New York, New York.

Bridge Game, 1948, page 51, courtesy of Martin Diamond Fine Arts, New York, New York.

When Winter Comes, 1924, page 73, courtesy of Sotheby's, New York, New York.

Shuffleton's Barbershop, 1950, page 74, courtesy of the Berkshire Museum, Pittsfield, Massachusetts.

The Music Lesson, 1921, page 77, courtesy of Berry-Hill Galleries, New York, New York.

Couple in Early Auto, 1924, page 93, courtesy of Christie's, New York, New York.

Couple in Rumbleseat, 1935, page 97, courtesy of Judy Goffman Fine Art, New York, New York.